ADVANCE PRAISE

Kinyamaswa is made powerful by its expansive landscape, dynamic lyricism, and striking imagery. Andreas Morgner has crafted a story of survival that brings history alive in startling rendition, recreating the dangerous and violent terrain in the aftermath of the 1994 Rwandan genocide. Pairing dream-like cantos with heartbreaking renderings of true events, Morgner allows readers to widen their realm of experience and compassion, thus deepening their understanding of the human condition. Robust storytelling and lyric power will propel you through this stark, yet deeply spiritual work. A timeless and artful investigation into the mutually assured costs of war.
 —Emily Stokes, managing editor, *Madcap Review*

Kinyamaswa bears itself as an immediately engaging, extremely interesting and painfully moving look at the social politics of genocide.
 —Kiran Tanna, Co-Director, York St John University Creative Press and Senior Editor, *Theatre Pages Magazine and Journal*

A great collection…brilliantly written.
 —S. D. Hintz, CEO, Bokalino Press

Fleeing the conventional through the forest of a classic form, Poet Andreas Morgner brings new purpose to the epic poem. Showing the heroism in small moments he takes the reader on a journey away from genocide to a greater awareness of how people survive each other. His command of details is subtle and stylish. The passing mention of color, noise, and casual gestures is beautifully poetic while the plot and pacing could compete with many popular novels.
 —Rebecca Wralstad, writer/film producer

Simply put, Morgner has a way with words. He employs truly beautiful and inspired language, but does not let it overshadow the refugees' poignant narrative. Their story is what shines here, and his poetry compliments and amplifies that story, just as poetry should.
—Samantha Molton, author

KINYAMASWA (MERCILESS)

Andreas Morgner

KINYAMASWA (MERCILESS)

Andreas Morgner

Apprentice House
Loyola University Maryland
Baltimore, Maryland

Copyright © 2015 by Andreas Morgner

All rights reserved. No part of this book may be reproduced or transmitted in any form or by any means, electronic or mechanical, including photocopy, recording, or any information storage and retrieval system, without prior permission from the publisher (except by reviewers who may quote brief passages).

First Edition

Printed in the United States of America
Paperback ISBN: 978-1-62720-074-5
E-book ISBN: 978-1-62720-075-2

Published by Apprentice House

Apprentice House
Loyola University Maryland
4501 N. Charles Street
Baltimore, MD 21210
410.617.5265 • 410.617.2198 (fax)
www.apprenticehouse.com
info@apprenticehouse.com

In Rwandan, *kinyamaswa* means "like an animal," but can also mean cruel, brutal, or ... *merciless*.

To exact revenge for yourself or your friends is not only a right,
it's an absolute duty.
— Stieg Larsson

To the last I grapple with thee; from hell's heart I stab at thee;
for hate's sake I spit my last breath at thee.
— Herman Melville, *Moby-Dick; or, The Whale*

If you need to injure someone, do it in such a way that you do not
have to fear their vengeance.
— Niccolò Machiavelli

I joined the army to avenge the deaths of my family and to survive, but I've come to learn that if I am going to take revenge, in that process I will kill another person whose family will want revenge; then revenge and revenge and revenge will never come to an end.
— Ishmael Beah, *A Long Way Gone:*
Memoirs of a Boy Soldier

ACKNOWLEDGMENTS

I would like to express my gratitude to the many people who saw me through this book: to all those who provided support, talked things over, read, wrote, offered comments, allowed me to quote their remarks, and assisted in the editing, proofreading, and design.

I would like to thank my wife, Mary, and the rest of my family, who supported and encouraged me in spite of all the time I was away from them.

I would also like to thank Jonathan Penton of Unlikely Books for his encouragement, which gave me the confidence to launch this project; John Lemon of Ilium Press, who gave me a much-needed and appreciated critique that helped me make this book what it is today; Apprentice House for being willing to take a chance on Kinyamaswa; Nicole Devincentis for cheerfully helping me to pull together all the bits and pieces that make up this book; Samantha Molton for the many hours she spent editing the manuscript so I could sound much smarter than I really am; and also Cheryle Linturn, Rebecca Wralstad, Carol Parris Krauss, Kiran Tanna, Theresa Johnson, Samantha Molton (again), and S. D. Hintz for their kind words.

Most of all, I want to thank you, the reader holding this book right now, for giving me time out of your busy life to share this journey. I hope you feel it is worth it.

AUTHOR'S NOTE

Pity this poor country. Nearly drowned in a sea of tears.
Twice unlucky in the thrusting insanity that
gripped its people. Two great tribes,
once peaceful neighbors, became bloody
enemies tearing at each other leaving

only the circling vultures content. How
many yesterdays were lost and
tomorrows forsworn. Blind hate,
nurtured by tribal leaders bent on
power was stoked until a spark, falling

from the night sky was all it took
to light a fire that consumed the
country. Battle and slaughter followed
where the wrong word on a *carte d'identit*é
meant death to countless thousands.

But the fortunes of war turned in favor of
the victims forcing those who thought all
questions could be answered with sharp steel
to flee their ancestral home for a new land.
A sea of haunted faces flowed across a line in

the road to anticipated safety. The guilty,
the complicit and the innocent would share
their misery in sweltering camps while war
pimps kept plotting and the night sky over
the border was lit by tracer rounds.

Yet vengeance would not be content to
wait for blind justice to shamble onto
the stage. A reckoning was coming on
swift wings. When it arrived, killers became
the prey under clouds gathered for

the second great bloodletting. The sea
flowed again, this time deep into dark
forests with ravenous triggers close behind.
Under the silent green canopy, cries for help went
unheard as implacable scores were settled.

This, then, is the story of some of those disappeared…

PROLOGUE

These are the hills behind the wars
waking each dawn to rise above the mists
and the smells that life—animal, flower,
fruit and human bestow upon the air.
Since God the Father opened His hands

to the new world He had created,
they have stood solid, immobile
upon roots thrust deep into the
valley soils. Ageless. Immortal.

Waiting.

Since before the first animal,
passed through the great forests,
that cloaked their broad flanks,

they waited;

or fish that swam across the
great lake from distant, rumored rivers
to the pebbled shores at their feet,

they waited;

or birds flew across skies still so new
that the winds had only just rustled their first leaves
and the first cloud shadow had not yet cooled their slopes,

they waited.

Biding their time for the arrival of Man. 59
The blessed child for whom all 60
on the earth, in the air and under 61
the deep waters had been created. 62
Through the years beyond counting 63

the hills stood in the silence that 64
reigned until the Father God gave the Word 65
and the ears of the first man and woman 66
opened at long last to finally hear 67
the beauty of their Creator's song. 68

While all of the gods could now look on 69
the land and marvel at its beauty, 70
even returning from their labors 71
occasionally to rest among the wonders 72
they had bestowed on this new world, 73

not all was as well as they had envisioned. 74

Some of the oldest tales handed down 75
from our elders' elders talk of a race of 76
mighty giants that existed before the rest of 77
creation arrived, perhaps even before 78
the gods themselves. Cold as the black wastes 79

that spawned them, they were envious 80
of what the gods had built and would not share. 81
Eventually, jealousy turned to hate and they tried to 82
seize this new dominion sparking a terrible war that 83
almost wrecked the cosmos. In the end, the gods 84

proved stronger and the giants were cast down,
falling from their ruined bastions to be sealed
forever in dark places deep underground
with the hills and mountains
marking their prisons.

Yet, in the depths of their misery of lost
glory and power, still the giants dreamed.
Storytellers point to the smoking hills and claim
that when the giants rage against their
bonds the earth groans, stones crack,

and the distant mountains burn with
fires thrown up from their struggles.
While securely bound, the stories warn,
the giants still seek revenge upon the gods'
creations, particularly Man, with whispers

that can travel through the walls
of rock to touch and poison minds.
Turning every man against his brother so that
the favorites of the gods will tear at each other
and this land given as a token of divine love

until the day comes when this Man-child,
in his blind, raging madness
so rends the earth and skies above
that the holy prisons will crumble and
the giants will be free once again

to reclaim their ancient kingdom.

CANTO I

The birds float up from giant trees with 111
the first staccato shots. Bullets flare 112
through orange flames, cleanly slicing 113
leaves to bury themselves in pale trunks, 114
brown dirt or red flesh. Mortar bombs 115

arc past clouds to blast the earth with 116
clawing barbarity. Again and again 117
the noise gathers itself into hard crests. 118
Then falls away into valleys of snapping 119
flames and cries of pain as the battle ebbs. 120

Eyes of stone knives cannot pierce 121
the acrid fog drifting ghostly through the brush. 122
Somewhere, a child cries plaintively. 123
Its thin voice singing past the moans of 124
the wounded. Only the still forms scattered 125

along the fringes of the camp are quiet. 126
Silent lips kissing the cool dirt. 127
The attack ends as quickly as it began 128
with only the thrashing leaves in the 129
forest marking the enemy's withdrawal. 130

He stands alone beside the languid river. 131
A tall man. Fraying uniform. Haunted eyes. 132
His formal rank meaningless, he is known 133
simply as "Commander" by his soldiers. 134
The echoing ring of the battle still loud 135

in his ears as his men prepare to move out.
Collecting gear, scavenging the dead.
He watches the rippling waters of the river
as they split, wrap around a boulder, then heal
themselves, leaving a small wake as a scar

stretching downstream until it is lost among
the scars from other rocks that breach
the surface or hide just out of sight.
The setting sun reflected in the undulating
shimmers keep him there transfixed until

a dark shape passes to break the spell. A body
caught in the current. Face up. Wearing the
uniform of an enemy soldier. The Commander
notes mildly the face is that of a boy's with lost
years forever separating him from the first shave

that would have welcomed him into manhood.
Wide eyes that should still be discovering the world
stare unseeing at the stars beginning to appear in the
darkening sky. Past the Commander the body slides
effortlessly downstream, bouncing ever-so-gently off

each rock it comes into contact with. How long,
he wonders, before this river merges with another,
perhaps one or two more before reaching the sea.
Will those eyes still be watching the cold stars
when they reach the endless waves of the ocean?

Will the clouds hang back so that the night sky 161
above will find its brother below in the water 162
giving this boy a bed of diamonds to rest on 163
while telling his sad tale over and again until 164
he disappears beyond distant horizons? 165

CANTO II

*Yes, we hated them, the Commander thought.
We were told their arrogance was so vast, their minds could
not embrace our humanity. We could not forget
the land they stole from us, the herds of cattle
trampling our hard-won farms, and, worst of all,*

*the accusing eyes of our cousins in '72, hands
bound, crocodile food floating in the Great Lake.
Ancient humiliations must be repaid, the radio
voices and politicians screeched. They laid the
shame of squandered generations heavy on our*

*backs and in our children's eyes. They poked at us
until our anger seethed behind daily smiles as we
yearned to call a debt for shed tears and cold waiting.
Common military victories would not be enough
to erase that stain. So ferocious were we for wronged*

*yesterdays, so mandatory was the justice of the act
that we could not be satisfied until we had taken
away all their tomorrows. Only in the glorious moment
when they were damned to the same purgatoried
history as our cheated forefathers and ours were*

*the only hands raised to the heavens above
would forgiveness be possible.*

But it was not to be...

Our future died in the same bloody dirt
as their women and children. We slaughtered
them in numbers that would have left the
night sky dark for want of stars to light our way
or beaches bereft of sand to hold back the surf.

Yet, still, we failed. We did not know nor
expect that their bloodied spirits would
add battalions to the strength of
their living fighters pouring across the land.
The arms that wielded machetes day and

night became too weak to pull triggers
so we were overrun in the middle of our
red madness. Broken, we had only one
choice. We ran and kept running until
our legs could no longer carry us. We

thought we were beyond the reach of
their ravenous vengeance in another
country but we didn't count on how their
anger would give them wings so that now
it is we, who dreamed such dark dreams

of a new era christened in blood,
that stand on the precipice.

CANTO III

211 Morning. The Commander's first sensation as he awakes
212 is a bug crawling across his face. Swiping it off,
213 he opens his eyes to stare up at the graying sky just
214 visible through the spears and shields of the leaves
215 above him. All around unseen people are stirring,

216 quiet voices a building murmur to the new day.
217 Standing, he sees very little of the humanity stretching
218 through the undergrowth he knows is spread across
219 the forest floor. Already their presence presses upon
220 him much as the growing humidity of the day. Of his own

221 soldiers he can only see a few immediately nearby.
222 Most are probably scattered among the civilians
223 where everyone dropped from exhaustion last night.
224 His own limbs complain with dull pulsing aches
225 from the punishment he gave them yesterday. Before

226 the war, most officers his age found comfort behind
227 desks leaving sweat and clutching mud behind with
228 their youth. Their greatest exercise was the walk to
229 Officers Club for evening drinks or to a local cabaret.
230 That life was now buried along with many of those

231 men. He stretches, feeling the years dragging
232 his bones, an insistent lover that would not be
233 denied her kiss. How easy, he thinks, to simply
234 go back to sleep, to become a clock with its
235 winding mechanism slowly, quietly, running down.

Yet still he lives. He wonders at his gift of survival
while others, so many others, are snatched by Death.
No family, friends, or even his classmates from the
l'École Militaire walk this path with him now,
each loss cutting one more connection to this world

until he feels adrift. His mind threatening to spin
out of control with nothing to hold him back, to anchor him.
Above, a lone bird whistles a tuneless melody calling,
calling with no answer returning through the leaves.
The smell of cooking food wafts past and he realizes

he is also very hungry. When had he last eaten? A day?
Two? The paunch from his staff headquarters days
long since disappeared and 2 new holes on his
belt mark the distance traveled from comfortable.
An orderly arrives with a tin of coffee. The bitter

scalding liquid helps bring the day into sharper focus.
He stares out over the underbrush where a fog
begins to form from the smoke of dozens of
cooking fires. Pans clatter as food is
prepared and people move about gathering

firewood. Some head downhill towards
the nearest stream with water jugs. He glances
up through the trees at the smoke wafts among
the branches of the forest canopy to catch the
first bright rays stroking the treetops. He begins

making mental notes of the scene. He silently considers
options as his fingers tap against his leg. Time to get
moving. He calls some of the nearest soldiers to him
and gives them orders. Some head off to other parts
of the camp. The Commander fills his canteen from

the water jug and grabs some spare ammunition
clips. Always busy so old bony secrets stay buried
deep in the past. After a quick meal, he collects
one of his sergeants, checks the time, and
marches into the brush.

CANTO IV

The border. Men trudge past, churning mud. 271
Boots grown to grotesque shapes by 272
clinging earth pulling at them as they wind 273
past abandoned vehicles, fuel exhausted or 274
engines broken by the strain of retreat. 275

Still hooked to some are artillery pieces. 276
The army's great symbols of iron virility lying 277
flaccid under their covers, left impotent 278
after ammo dumps were abandoned, barrels pointing 279
shamefully towards the earth, drained of power 280

when most needed under an apricot sunrise. 281
Past the border guards, many drop rifles 282
or, if milice, machetes and clubs. 283
Officers shout to maintain order but 284
exhaustion commands now along with 285

relief that the race is over. These are 286
not the proud soldiers that strutted 287
arrogantly on distant parade grounds. 288
Most of those men are gone. 289
Dead or lost along hundreds of 290

kilometers of road or battlefields 291
that were never named. Even when 292
the faces are the same, the starched 293
uniforms of ceremonies are now worn 294
into shreds, scraps, ghosts of uniforms 295

mixed with whatever else they could find
along the many paths to this ending.
Some faces are entirely new. Old men
and those too young to have ever scraped
a razor across naked skin still yearning for

schoolyard play. Now these boys own
their killers' faces adding years to their walk.
Some have already taken wives from the
crowds of refugees who are themselves no
more than girls grown old and hard with

eyes that speak of things that most adults
never see or would want to see. The young
now fight their parents' battles. The living
take up the baton to fight for the dead.
For them, words like "peace" or "rich,"

would always be from a foreign language.

CANTO V

Claudine woke suddenly as the Commander
strode by. His boots nearly brushed her head
where she and her friend Esther lay curled
under a bush where they had crawled
when the soldiers finally called a halt.

If her feet didn't ache she would have
thought it just a terrible dream. How long
did they walk she couldn't say. Maybe just
hours but it felt like weeks since starting
out the previous day and then all night

in near-total darkness. One hand on
the person in front of you, staying quiet
even as gunfire beat the air all around.
Now daylight returned to push the nightmare
back for awhile, breathing the colors back into

the world. As she watched Esther's face
return to life as the growing light shifted
the gray pallor of the fitful predawn light to
warm hues of sunlight. Claudine gave a small prayer
of thanks they made it this far while unpacking

her bundle. As in the camp, she took up the
hard work of daily living. Every act of preparing
food, binding blistered feet, using a little of their
precious water to wash off some of the grime,
a personal incantation to the new day,

part of the perpetual hunt by all refugees
for a fragile balance when Hope is a
hungry animal surviving on crumbs.
Esther sat up, stretched, and flashed a
brilliant smile at Claudine. The two women

had first met in the camp, amputated from
families, needing to make new ties,
creating a new whole stitched over old stumps.
Exorcising their demons, singing back
the silence, the deafness to keep from

drifting back into a kind of vacant numbness.
Throwing themselves into their work,
running a makeshift clinic with sporadic
help from aid groups and doctors drifting
through to appease the endemic guilt of the

haves with a brief stint of band-aid care.
The two women became inseparable, leaning
on each other through the epidemics and
food shortages, later to make good their
harrowing escape after the camp came

under attack. Encouraging each other
to keep up with the column as it hurried
through the night. Trying not to panic knowing
those unseen hunters were sometimes close.
Very close. Imagined hands reaching

for them. Clutching. Straining fingers
almost brushing their hair…

CANTO VI

They left the camp, shrouded in the smoke 364
of burning tents and grass huts. The fight 365
was over but more attacks were certain. 366
Evacuation the only option. The soldiers 367
set fire to everything they could hoping 368

the smoke would mask their departure 369
long enough to get a head start. 370
Following a path that kept the smoke between 371
them and the hills where the enemy troops 372
watched with seething hunger, she tried 373

not to look at the rows of still forms bundled 374
under straw mats or multicolored cloth 375
that flapped in the breeze. A final farewell 376
wave to the living? Or were they beckoning 377
us to stay and join them? 378

CANTO VII

379 It was almost noon before the Commander
380 returned. His headquarters, only a small
381 clearing, was now filled with soldiers
382 talking, cleaning their weapons while
383 women chattered while they cooked the

384 morning meal. Soon, the other officers
385 arrived. Two were regular military.
386 He knew their worth from months of
387 fighting. The other, the milice leader
388 Colonel Runihura, a small mountain on legs

389 whose cruel face was only somewhat softened
390 by tortoiseshell glasses, was the last to appear.
391 The meeting went quickly. Congratulations
392 were offered to the military men for their
393 troops' bravery and their own skill in

394 conducting a fighting retreat in the dark
395 until the enemy gave up the chase. Now
396 came the hard part.

397 They could not stay.

398 Another attack was imminent. The Commander
399 had seen a large enemy force camped a few
400 kilometers away. There was no one to turn
401 to for help. While in camp, indolent
402 peacekeepers and sanctimonious aid groups

had done nothing to stop the attack. Hundreds
died while the West turned its face away in
passive judgment, a silent verdict, and
now a voyeuristic execution. More enemy
reinforcements were undoubtedly coming.

To stay meant a fight they could not
win and a slaughter of the civilians out
of sight of the world media. The only option,
make for the nearest government-held
town four day's march away. To better

their chances, the refugees and the attached
military units would be split into three
columns under the leadership of the
surviving officers. Runihura would fold what's
left of his milice into the Commander's unit.

The milice man was incensed at this loss
of status but his group was now the smallest
contingent. Muttering over his lost status,
he stomped off to his men while the military
officers plotted routes and strategies. A

final farewell salute and wishes for
luck ended the meeting.

The Commander then called his sergeants
together to outline his plan. Soon his
soldiers were packing whatever supplies
could fit in their backpacks or could be
carried by their women or men pressed

into service as porters. Others began
moving through the crowd of refugees
passing along the instructions:

Drop anything that's not vital.

Everyone must keep up the pace.

Anyone unable to will be left behind.

While listening to his orders being relayed,
the Commander thought back to school when
he first learned about Charles Darwin.
Survival of the fittest he thought,
We are going to practice that now.

CANTO VIII

The tribe's memory is in the land 441
it swims deep in the blood. 442
Voices are buried in each layer of dirt. 443
Our ancestors' bones still tell the old stories 444
and children yet unborn whisper what is to come. 445

Each rock a parable, every boulder a legend. 446
Bonds that tie the tribe to its home. 447
Listen. Can you hear them talking? 448
In the old days, the elders would take the children 449
to the caves up in the hills where paintings 450

could still be seen imparting their knowledge 451
of the land and how it provides for its people. 452
Hunters with faces of lions and birds, living so close 453
to the forest animals that lines dividing species blurred. 454
The spirits of our ancestors wearing feathers 455

hovering over the buffalo and gazelle 456
guiding them to our arrows. Back in the village, 457
on moonless night with the stars run riot, 458
the Old Ones still join us in the tribe's dances 459
to hear their descendants both young and old 460

telling the tales first spoken so long ago 461
before returning to their silvery homes 462
across the dark, dark ocean. 463

CANTO IX

464 Claudine and Esther finished their packing.
465 They walked to where the soldiers were
466 waving their arms urging people to get
467 moving. The two women joined the
468 general flow into a small valley at the edge

469 of the camp. There the soldiers and officers
470 were forcing people into three lines. As the
471 crowd shuffled along, they ignored a
472 nearly naked woman dancing, shaking loose
473 a memory filling her empty arms with a lost

474 lover and her ears with the sweet music of
475 gentle words long gone. Esther watched her
476 waltz until the vision was lost among the
477 sweaty, anxious faces around her. Claudine
478 took Esther's hand as they neared where

479 the sorting was taking place. Some families
480 being separated as the soldiers tried to even
481 the numbers. There were some raised voices
482 and crying but the almost palpable fear
483 coursing through the struggling mass of

484 people was an invisible whip urging them on.
485 Beyond the sorting area Claudine could see
486 people dashing from one group to another
487 to rejoin loved ones anyway. The long
488 lines of people were moving now,

multicolored streams flowing among
the trees. Their heads hidden under food
sacks, bedding, children, even
sheets of roofing tin for the houses some
felt sure they would be building someday.

Each new river of bodies already forming
its own swirls of energy that rose out of
their accumulated fears to add their own
particular thrummings to the rumbling beat of
thousands of feet on the forest floor.

Claudine kept her eyes on the ground as
slick mud, roots, and vines threatened to
trip her. By the time they had reached a
game trail and the going got easier, she
realized with a start that the forest had already

swallowed up the other two columns.

CANTO X

On her ward, one of the patients burned
with fever, his face shining with sweat.
Cancer ate at him and over several months
she had watched him fade over many
visits into the ghostly figure that barely

left a ripple under the sheets. The grin he
always met her with tore her heart knowing
his pain. Yet he was always kind and
talked as if they were meeting at a bistro
downtown rather than at his deathbed.

He spoke of running away as a young boy
from his father's farm to become a sailor.
Working on Arab dhows that plied the
vast stretches of water between the Gulf
and the African coast. She loved his stories

of exotic ports, smuggling, and the people
he had known. Each tale a tender touch,
a lover's opening move. She could feel the
breeze in her face and almost smell the spice
markets she had never visited from his words.

At other times he would fill her ears with the
remembered creak of wood shifting as the wind caught
the sails. Her eyes saw dolphins racing the ship
then leaping into the air in fountains of spray
offering to share their simple joy.

*Finally, with pain beyond endurance
and medicines ineffective, the day came
when he asked her to scatter his ashes
with the wind on the Great Lake. That
was the last time she saw him.*

*Before she could fulfill her last promise,
the killings began and the hospital was
one of the first targets for the milice.*

CANTO XI

538 Nearby, Father Pierre is helping several families
539 sort what belongings were rescued from the camp.
540 Little time was given before they had to leave.
541 Everyone frantic to go but also afraid of what
542 might be waiting in the forest. He went among

543 his flock helping where he could, offering advice
544 to others. The group had grown while in the camp.
545 The ranks of those that survived the trek with
546 him when the *ancien régime* collapsed swelled
547 with newer refugees that trickled in later. Now

548 exhausted and fewer in number with some lost
549 in the confusion of the battle and the night march,
550 they went about their preparations arthritically.
551 When he could, he said a quiet prayer for the
552 safety of those missing he hoped were still alive

553 but included a plea for their souls if they weren't.
554 Around him his parishioners finished their
555 sorting and began moving to the assembly point.
556 They all knew the score from bitter experience.

557 Keep moving to live.

558 They had fled their homes as the war swept across
559 the land. Trekking hundreds of miles into this remote
560 region of another country where the local tribes were
561 allied with their enemies. Hostility and suspicion

drove them into overcrowded camps indifferently
managed by outsiders. Little food. Daily stench
of raw sewage. Rampant disease. Lost hope.
Thousands died who survived the guns.
Now just as aid had begun to flow in amounts

that allowed conditions to improve, the guns
returned to finish the job. Faces that Father Pierre
knew since birth now were aging quickly. The
few children left seemed old with innocence an
early casualty. Each possessing an intimacy

with Pain, that rough lover, the handmaiden
of every conflict where blood is spilled from
house to house, across playgrounds, schools
and casual dreams that once clothed the future
in shining raiments. Now eyes are cast down

to a tattered reality where safety is a fading
memory and everyone's focus is simply
to live another day.

CANTO XII

580 *The machete was a natural tool for us.*
581 *Many used it daily cutting sugarcane,*
582 *chopping firewood, killing chickens*
583 *until the heft of the steel blade, the*
584 *way the handle molded to your grip,*

585 *made it a natural extension of your arm.*
586 *Each swing moving with an easy grace*
587 *the blade biting deeply every time.*
588 *So second nature to your body that*
589 *the hours slid off muscles as easily as sweat*

590 *on a hot day harvesting in the fields.*
591 *For many, the impact jarring the metal and*
592 *wood handle barely registered past bone and*
593 *sinew on into the recesses of the mind,*
594 *the rhythm of the job becoming a trance*

595 *from which we did not, could not awake.*

596
597 *Some became the blade during the*
598 *cuttings, breeding a hunger that only*
599 *grew with each new kill. The steel had*
600 *its own will pulling legs and minds along*
601 *through long days searching brush,*

abandoned farms, swamps of 602
sucking mud and scraping papyrus. 603
These predators became dangerous 604
even to us, their longtime friends, 605
madness building behind wide eyes 606

until only blood, any blood would do. 607
On the hunt, they howled their lust 608
as their quarry was flushed into the open. 609
Later, it took soothing words and many 610
cold beers at the evening's gathering 611

to quiet their feral hearts to find 612
the men they used to be. 613

The shouters from the cities didn't 614
have to push us to do this work. 615
We all knew what had to be done, 616
how what was begun in anger later 617
became a chore that needed doing 618

like any other on the farm as days 619
stretched into weeks, finally 620
becoming a rush to complete quickly. 621
Don't dawdle, everyone must help, 622
the local bosses said rolling up their sleeves. 623

Leave the looting to the women they scolded. 624
Later, there will be plenty to share 625
once the last of those insects are gone. 626
So hurry, hurry now, push on! 627
Forget aching muscles, blistered hands. 628

Ignore your rumbling bellies.
Keep your eyes and ears open
and your blades sharp.

They are still out there in the forests.
Hiding. Running. Watching.
Covered in mud, almost invisible now.
Learning from the wild animals.
using the night as a cloak

just beyond the light of our fires.
Becoming the mist in the morning
to slip through our lines. We have to finish it
now. Do not leave their unspilled blood
to become the ink to record our deeds.

So hurry, hurry now, push on!
Forget aching muscles, blistered hands.
Ignore that rumbling you hear,
the thunder that goes on and on
as artillery climbs distant hills.

—Conseiller, 37

CANTO XIII

The Commander had to organize his soldiers
on the fly. He broke them into three sections
under sergeants he trusted.   One at the head
of the column, one at the rear, and the last unit
placed in the middle as a reserve.   The remnants

of Runihura's gendarmerie he parceled out among his
soldiers. They were largely untrained as soldiers
and unarmed, having thrown away the machetes
and clubs that were their trademarks. The Commander
ordered his own men to teach them as much of the

basics of infantry fighting as they could on the way.
His fear was that, like in the camp, as soon as the
bullets started flying, so would they.   He saw Runihura
walking in the column with his heavily armed personal
guard. Behind the gendarmerie leader's entourage were

dozens of people the Commander could see had been
pressed into service as the milice's porters. The
Commander walked past Runihura without acknowledging
his presence and moved to the front of the column.

With his usual long strides, the Commander moved
alongside the trudging masses who moved at a pace that
would seem leisurely if he did not already know how
worn most people felt, how many were already weak
from hunger, from disease, from fear when they

abandoned the camp. Pushing bicycles or stooped
under bundles that looked like they could break
the back of a horse they still moved steadily.
Only time would tell who had the strength to persevere.
He passed many close enough to touch them but his

eyes looked past to the path ahead and on through the
forest to the miles beyond that they had yet to travel. It
was in this detached state that he almost walked by her.
He snapped out of his reverie at the last moment at the
sight of a red bandana with a familiar floral pattern.

He slowed his pace to walk a few paces behind her.
It was Claudine, that nurse who bravely ran the
makeshift clinic back in camp. He had spoken to her
on a few occasions when some of his men needed
treating or when she came to the camp management

meetings to push for better sanitation or more
antibiotiques to treat the sick. A quiet girl who
spoke with an inner strength that made people
listen more than if she yelled and stamped her feet.
He had always liked talking to her, the natural

optimism she harbored made what some saw as
impossible only a nuisance to be overcome. Her
smile shining in the sepia glow of the camp lanterns.
Her face throwing off its own light the same way
a diamond multiplies the light thrown at it,

giving birth to a kaleidoscope of hearts and arrows,
inventing new colors. Now she walked alongside that
girl from the Interior Ministry. Those two had seemed
inseparable to the point he had once wondered if
there was ever any room in her life for a man.

He hesitated opening his mouth and actually thought
of picking up his pace to pass her as if he hadn't seen
her when she suddenly turned and looked straight at him.
He laughed as she ran up and threw her arms around him.
You're alive she laughed, stepping back after a moment

as the other girl (he suddenly remembered her name
was Esther) also gave him a more sedate hug.
Immediately Claudine launched into a breathless swirl
of questions and stories that the Commander barely
heard. The words cascading past him much too fast

to catch hold. He smiled and held his hands up in
mute surrender as two of his sergeants approached
with frowns on their faces. *I wish I could stay and
talk with you but duty calls. We can catch up later.
I'm just so glad you two made it.* Abruptly, on their

own accord, his hands reached and took ahold of hers.
A quick squeeze and he turned to leave. Claudine and
Esther watched his quick retreat for a few moments
before rejoining the column. They whispered and giggled
as they walked, not noticing the flat stare locked

on them nearby. Runihura, approaching with his men, had watched their meeting with the Commander. His broad face, which had been surly with the discomfort of the walk, now started to break into a smile.

CANTO XIV

My sister's wedding was the last
traditional feast I was able to
celebrate before leaving to join
the army. Men and women of
the village had spent days gathering

food and then two more cooking it in
dozens of large pots set up in the
open area of the family compound.
Girls and boys shuttled to the
stream for water. Since I was older,

I could go with the men to split
and stack firewood. I was so happy
to be part of their world that it barely
felt the like work even though I spent
several hours in the sun swinging my

father's axe. The elders who were
too old to work but told stories, later
praised me for my stamina and made
sly remarks that my future wife would
appreciate it. Back at the compound,

goats were slaughtered and their meat
was fed into vats of soup. Soon the
bride's family arrived bringing many
pots of palm wine which, like the food,
disappeared quickly between happy lips.

*Later, there was dancing both for the
men and women. When I was a child,
I had always watched how the men
danced, acting out legends of the gods
and giants. Of snake spirits and demons.*

*Of those that protected and those that
would lure a man to his doom far from
any help. I watched every move closely
memorizing them for the day I would
stand in the center of the crowd and*

*every eye was on me. This last time was
different. I still enjoyed the stories but now
I found myself much more interested in
the women's dances. I could not tear my
eyes away from the girls who were my age.*

*I must have been pretty obvious because
they often gave me funny looks in return.
Some just shy peeks. Others not so shy.
Each one stole the air from my lungs.
Their swaying hips that moved in time*

*to the drums set my heart on fire under
the stars. I wanted the night to go on
and one of those girls to become mine
before the dawn but I drank too much
palm wine and woke up the next morning*

*alone next to the village stream.
Now with everyone scattered, I guess
I will never get to dance.*

—Soldier, 17

CANTO XV

Throughout the long day's march, 781
Father Pierre badly wanted to sing 782
some hymns to lift his people's 783
spirits. The soldiers, ever tense, were 784
going up and down the column hushing 785

everyone. The fear was infectious. 786
Eyes darted over every shadow or 787
movement in the forest. Hands 788
clamped tight over mouths wanting to 789
cough or babies whimpering themselves 790

into full-throated cries. The old priest 791
even tried humming to himself but 792
sharp stares and fingers on lips from 793
those around made him stop. All he 794
could think of doing was whispering 795

his daily office under his breath, chanting 796
well-worn prayers to the beat of his stride. 797
When he finished Terce, he tried to pray again 798
for divine forgiveness for him and his flock. 799
Instead of redemption, memories flooded in. 800

Crystal clear shards stabbing behind his eyes. 801
These were of a different group of desperate 802
refugees. Clustered on the doorstep of his 803
church the night the Cuttings began. 804
Interrupting his quiet reflection of the Book 805

of Revelations. Begging for help through
the wood of the door, for protection from
the killers whose searing headlights and
whistles were approaching from the valley.
He knew no one who gave them shelter

would be spared. So he fled, Holy Book
in hand to protect him from this satanic
madness, a miasma rising out of the
swamp in choking clouds of old hatreds.
He burst out the back door stumbling,

running into the moonlight but not
fast enough to take him out of
earshot before the screaming started.
The shame made him clutch his crucifix
so tightly that he felt something warm

and wet run down his fingers before
he felt the pain. A hand gently touched
his shoulder. Lysette, his deacon's
widow, was there giving him a worried
look. He managed a wan smile but

could not speak as he was afraid he
would howl uncontrollably if he
opened his mouth. *We all have our*
nightmares now, mon Pere she said.
Lysette took off her head scarf

to bind his hand. Still unable to speak,
he walked on in silence with unseeing
eyes through the indifferent forest.

CANTO XVI

Beyond the circle of faces glowing in
the dim yellow light of an old oil lamp,
masses of insects communicated their
frenzied ecstasy with a shrill whine.
The darkness, as he walked among the

clustered groups, felt solid and impenetrable,
a mountain that rested heavily on the
forest canopy looming, stretching above
their heads barely pierced by the scattered
lamps and fires. Most of the faces were

quiet but here and there were voices,
words spoken with the easy cadence that
storytellers use for the old familiar fables that
can push back the night for a while and give
wings to minds eager to fly beyond empty

stomachs and blistered feet. The movements
of each fire's retinue casting huge shadows
against the trees, bringing to life old tales
of the gods and giants who ruled
these lands in dimly imagined days

while the forest's inhabitants lurked beyond the light,
filling the darkness with their clamor. So unlike
back home where the animals had left the uneasy hills
shuddering in their deep pain, occasionally vomiting
clouds of foul smoke into the unsuspecting air.

CANTO XVII

859 They walked through the jungle
860 and clearings towards a ridge
861 of hills that beckoned them.
862 You can go further, always farther,
863 it's not far, the clouds passing

864 overhead whispered urging them on.
865 The lights and shadows clothing each
866 person in turn with the same pattern
867 as they passed underneath the canopy.
868 Birds in the trees whistled and chattered

869 as they discussed the intrusion.
870 The column paid them no attention
871 eyes cast down to the path,
872 backs bent to the weight of their packs.
873 Only the soldiers posting themselves

874 on high points, looked beyond the path
875 eyes intently scanning the way ahead for
876 obstacles and the woods behind
877 for any signs of pursuit. Sometimes
878 there would be places where

879 everything became utterly still as if
880 all that ever needed to be said by animals
881 wind and trees had already been said.
882 A hush that took in every ebb and flow,
883 folding into itself every sound so that

even the beat of hundreds of feet or
the labored breaths they took were lost in the
stillness until a single cough, a snapping
stick, or the sigh of a breeze reborn
broke the spell releasing the imprisoned

noises back into the waiting air. The hours
wore on as the forests marched past
until even the roots that stretched across
the path all looked the same as if they were
walking in place.   Only the occasional stream

offered any respite with cooling waters that
blessed sore feet and parched throats. Stops
were infrequent and when the word came to resume
the march after each all-too-brief rest, people
would climb stiffly to their feet, an army of the

resurrected dead rising ever-so-reluctantly
from beds of soothing earth into the
dreaded pains of renewed life.
Slowly, eventually, as the hours passed,
shadows began to lengthen along the path

as the sun sank towards the great treetops
that canopied the way ahead of them.
Spearing their eyes with sharp light
wherever the trees held back their
branches over the path and the

909 undergrowth withdrew in its
910 genuflection to the day's passage.
911 The shadows were loosening up
912 from their slumber during the
913 day's heat and readying themselves

914 for when they soon would dance
915 with the Great Dark to rule the land.
916 With a large hill looming overhead
917 the trees suddenly fell away to bare
918 ground turned to stone, etched

919 by ancient floods and cracked by
920 the heat of a thousand droughts.
921 Turning south, they followed the
922 dropping ground into a ravine
923 where a stream slid past rocks

924 pried loose from the rising cliffs
925 on either side. The pebbled streambed
926 nestled the swift waters sliding quickly
927 over scattered golden flecks peeking
928 from among their duller cousins.

929 Unseeing, unknowing callused feet
930 trod them deeper into the muck
931 kicked up by their headlong passage.
932 The stream dropped into a valley
933 and hooked to one side leaving a

pasture strewn with debris from past 934
floods. There, orders were given and 935
the column slowed as it spread, 936
flooding the pasture. Filling it, 937
spreading across the grass until 938

it filled the meadow right up to 939
the edge of the forest beyond, 940
lapping against the great trunks. 941
People stopping, laying out their homes for 942
the night. Soldiers piled kindling, 943

an experimental fire was started. 944
When the dry wood offered no 945
tell-tale smoke, dozens of other 946
fires were soon going… 947

Despite aching muscles protesting 948
every step, the Commander climbed a hill 949
overlooking the camp with some of 950
his sergeants. There he took out his 951
binoculars to look out over the 952

scattered fires below him and on to 953
the hills purpling in the day's dying light. 954
His soldiers sat or lay in the grass, 955
resting from the long march. Few spoke. 956
All were waiting for the commands 957

that would wrap up the day. Before 958
they got too comfortable, the Commander 959
began pointing out where to set up guard posts 960
along possible approaches into the valley. 961
Shifts were organized. Rations and ammunition 962

assigned. Then they left. He remained,
staring into the gathering gloom.
They were his men. His boys. The sons
he never had who he led and even
ordered to their deaths if the need arose.

They trusted him as had so many before
who lay all but forgotten in the dark red
soil of their lost homeland. How many
more from what he still had left? Some?
Most? All? He used to know all the men

he led. Now it seemed hardly worth the effort
as few lasted long. Now all that mattered was
to get these civilians to safety. These last
ragged survivors of a once mighty tribe.
He wondered how the other columns were

doing as he stared out over the distant hills.
Fold following fold on into the misty distance.
Sighing, he put away the binoculars. He
didn't need them anymore. He could
clearly see the flickering lights leaking

from between the trees on several distant
hilltops, announcing the bold watch fires
being lit by the enemy.

CANTO XVIII

When we left our homeland with fear   986
lashing our feet, I looked back and   987
saw them outlined on the last ridge   988
at the border. Tall, gaunt figures   989
standing silently against the sky.   990

The wizards of the old stories   991
watching their magic take shape   992
in the defeat of ancient enemies.   993

CANTO XIX

994 The smell of burning wood and cooking food was
995 slowly winning over the smells of overworked
996 bodies and the tang of fear in the breeze,
997 that overflowing black cup all drank from
998 that quenched no thirst nor filled any belly.

999 Claudine ate her soup quietly with Esther and
1000 several other women who had gravitated to them
1001 sharing their paltry supplies for this evening meal.
1002 In actuality, for most of them, this was the only
1003 meal for the day making every morsel precious.

1004 Little was said so the scrape of spoons in bowls,
1005 the rustle of cloth when they moved and the crackling
1006 fire seemed loud. Around them there was little talk among
1007 the other groups as they stared into their campfires. When
1008 someone spoke, it was only in hushed church whispers.

1009 Only across the camp, where the milice had gathered
1010 was there noise. Talking. Laughter. A tinny song
1011 blared from a stereo. A dance tune but no one was
1012 moving. The tone of their party was one of desperate
1013 enjoyment against what might be hiding in the silence.

1014 For Claudine, what WAS in the languid air was a low hum.
1015 A sound that seemed to be coming from every person around her.
1016 An echo left behind from every grain of gun powder
1017 burned, every heart shattered forever, every drop of blood
1018 dried into the dirt, and every bed left empty.

Even as she hung the dirty white sheet with a red
cross painted crudely on it. Even as the first patients
stumbled or were carried in, it was there. A noise
that drew her back into herself. It was another person
examining these people, giving the other women tasks,

binding injuries. She floated somewhere behind
those eyes watching all this. It was a movie she longed
to turn off. To sleep or to wander away. Perhaps
into the forest. To see something untouched by
the war. Even if only a small flower clinging to

a vine that had never been seen by Man. A species
with no name in a book to define it. A stranger
that simply was and had no ambition to be anything
else. From that, she would look for others who knew
nothing of what had happened. More plants.

Animals. Mountains. Lakes. Until she had found
enough of everything to build a new world with
no ties to the one she had been born into. A garden
where the snake and apple never found their way
in and the first tear had yet to be shed.

It was in this state, as her body performed its
tasks and her mouth formed words to comfort
a pregnant woman that the outside world intruded
when a hand suddenly appeared on her shoulder.
The surprise was electric, slamming her back

into her body, her soul slotting itself once again against her skin. She turned and saw the Commander standing over her with a questioning look on his face. She could not help but smile. His was a face, strained as it was under the burdens of his station,

that had the rare gift of being made kinder by this war's many horrors rather than crueler like so many others. As always when he visited he was carrying a gift. A dull green canvas bag blazoned with a bright red cross. She quickly grabbed it and opened the flap.

It was packed with dressings, medicines, various salves, and an assortment of medical instruments. A treasure for their little *clinique*. She stood, laughing and gave him a kiss on the cheek. *As always, my angel* she said excitedly looking again at her prize. *This will help so much. We have had nothing but rags to bind wounds since we left the camp.* He smiled, *I thought you could use some help. I wish we could do more but our supplies are almost gone too. We'll all just have to make do until we reach the garrison.*

Well, this is still better than what we had a minute ago So, again, thanks. She turned and handed the bag to one of her helpers. When she turned to face him again, he was checking his watch. *You won't stay?* she asked. He grinned, *I would love to but I have to check on the guard posts to make sure the watches are set. I will try to look in on you tomorrow if I can. We will be starting out again early so be ready to move out with your patients as soon as it is light.* Can't we stay a little longer? she pleaded. *Everyone is so tired.*

I wish we could, he sighed, *I could sleep for a week myself but our friends*—he waved in the direction where he had seen the watch fires—*are certain to be here by midday so I want to be as far away as possible by then.* He took her hand. *If I get the chance, I'll check in on you again. I promise.*

He let go of her hand and put his cap back on. He smiled again, *Get as much rest as you can, it will be a long march tomorrow. Adieu.* She watched him go, wishing he would find some reason to turn back around but he soon was out of sight.

CANTO XX

1084 *In the hush of the day's growing light*
1085 *at the edge of the forest giants,*
1086 *dry leaves cloak the growing season's*
1087 *bounty in the cool morning mist.*
1088 *Still holding the trees back from*

1089 *ancient fields, the rock wall stands.*
1090 *Where once hands as rough and strong*
1091 *as they laid these stones out.*
1092 *One rock on two, two on one.*
1093 *By look and feel they were fitted*

1094 *that season long ago when the field*
1095 *was first wrested from boulders*
1096 *and stumps. No mortar used,*
1097 *only gravity and friction holding tight*
1098 *the many becoming fused as if one.*

1099 *Unbreakable through decades of*
1100 *farm work it stood watching*
1101 *as crops were sown and*
1102 *later, the harvests brought in.*
1103 *Families came, grew tall, and*

1104 *dimmed towards final goodbyes.*
1105 *Even after faces turned towards*
1106 *the bright lights on distant horizons,*
1107 *the wall kept its vigil as straight*
1108 *furrows disappeared under meadow*

grasses and later tangled brush 1109
while small animals made the wall 1110
their home and accepted without 1111
question the unsown bounty the 1112
land, sun, and rains provided. 1113

Yet still the wall endured. 1114
Waiting with infinite patience 1115
for the iron plows and those rough, 1116
familiar hands which gave it birth 1117
to, at long last, return. 1118

CANTO XXI

1119 When the night had grown stale and the hint
1120 of the coming sun began to outline the hills,
1121 the word spread to move out. No order rang out
1122 only a nearly wordless stirring that spread in a wave
1123 among the huddled forms, flowing around embered fires.

1124 Father Pierre found himself upright and slipping
1125 the straps of his pack over his shoulders before he
1126 was fully awake. The activity across the camp
1127 numb, mechanical. An army of robots being
1128 switched on. Seemingly chaotic movements belied

1129 its sharp focus. The kind that comes as petty
1130 ambitions and jealousies are forgotten. Each mind
1131 folding itself into a single point. No past. No future.
1132 Only here. Only now. A lifetime now defined by the
1133 task at hand. The horizon confined to the nearest faces.

1134 Yet nearby, Father Pierre noticed a single oasis
1135 of stillness. A woman lay unmoving with a small
1136 girl cradling her head on a tiny lap. A hand rose
1137 tentatively to clasp the child. Words were softly
1138 spoken. Then, as if a string was cut, the woman's

1139 hand dropped. The child leaned closer, wrapping
1140 her arms around the woman's head. Her tiny
1141 voice trying to call back a spirit already flying
1142 up to the backlit clouds above. Father Pierre
1143 could only watch as this small tragedy unfolded.

Before he could rouse himself, a young couple stepped out from the crowds around them. The woman bent over and whispered into the little girl's ear. The girl turned, face wet with tears, held out her arms, and let the woman pick her up. The young man picked up the dead woman's

bundle and threw it over his shoulder. They then walked quietly into the mass of humanity and disappeared as another man strode up and laid a blanket over the body. Released from his paralysis, Father Pierre knelt over the body and began reciting the Last Rites as he realized

he had just watched a new family being born.

CANTO XXII

A small bundle is handed out of the hut
where the women have crowded waiting
for hours. Eyes that have seen dark times
and the heavy toll of many tears now grow bright
as a small cry begins. A delicate, fragile

sound that begs for arms to fold it close
with the warm embrace of a womb. Under the
branches of a great tree that has seen this many
times before, the bundle illuminates the
shadows as it is presented to the extended clan.

Each person, in turn, offers a greeting.
A chant begins and a drum is tapped
while plates of food arrive from the
cooking pits. A song has started that one day
this child will teach us how to sing.

With a smile and an open heart,
I welcome you, granddaughter.

CANTO XXIII

Dawn found the column already on its way. Not
until the sun was nearly at peak did the Commander
call for a rest. Everyone immediately collapsed
where they stopped. While soldiers kept watch
Claudine and Esther unwrapped their bundles and

brought out dried fish along with some spices to cut
the vile taste. They spoke lightly of their lives
before the war. They were so occupied that they
didn't notice Runihura and his guards approaching
until they stood right over them. He pointed at Claudine.

You come with me. You're my cook now.
Runihura then reached down to haul Claudine
to her feet with one powerful hand and started
dragging her towards the underbrush. Now
thoroughly frightened, Claudine started screaming

Stop it. I don't want to go with you. Help me.
Runihura's guards laughed and brandished their
guns at the people nearby to emphasize their power.
He was almost at the bushes with his prize when a
voice asked calmly, *Is there a problem here?*

Startled, Runihura turned to find the Commander
standing calmly with a squad of soldiers behind him.
He was so distracted he let go of Claudine's arm.
She retreated out of reach and stood shivering.

Runihura declared loudly, *I am an important member of the milice and an advisor to the Ruling Council. I have the right to any woman I want.* The Commander stared at Runihura steadily. *I don't care what position you held before or whose*

ass you licked back in the capital. Here I command. No one has the right to abuse any of the civilians under my protection. Cause another scene like this and I will have my men tie you and any of your goons who want to share your fate, to the nearest

tree and leave you as a present for our pursuers. With that the Commander turned and walked towards the head of the column. Claudine ran over to Esther, in a couple of heartbeats they gathered their belongings and ran after the Commander.

Thank you, thank you Claudine said breathlessly when she caught up to him. *I did that for everyone in the column* he replied keeping his eyes forward *that kind of behavior could endanger us all.* He glanced at her, *for your own safety I think you*

should stay near my men at front and well away from that swine. Now I have work to do he said. He picked up his pace and with his squad, headed off to check on his sentries. Claudine watched him disappear into the brush for a moment then

moved quickly towards the front of the column with Esther.

CANTO XXIV

Sitting on the verandah of his house
dressed in white, sipping a rare malt,
the Politician watches as gardeners'
clippers keep the flowering bougainvillea
from ruining his view of the placid waters

of the Great Lake and the terraced slopes rising
beyond. He crosses his legs and sighs
wearily at the intrusion of the question.
Righteous angels or psychopathic demons,
it's all the same when it comes to a society's

warriors. They have to kill to win victories.
If successful, the harm to the innocent is
rarely questioned. Massacre or collateral
damage. It is all semantics for the history
books. Few spare any thought for what

this does to the soul of a soldier—whether
he is a man or boy—except for those
interfering foreign do-gooders.
He is merely a tool to be used and
thrown away if necessary…

Melting ice tinkles in the glass.

After all, the Politician concludes,
who really cares for the feelings of
a hammer or an axe?

CANTO XXV

1247 After an hour, the signal came to resume
1248 the march. In minutes, the kilometer-long
1249 snake was again winding through the forest.
1250 The shadows were starting to lengthen
1251 when the drone of an aircraft was heard.

1252 Everyone froze as it circled lazily overhead
1253 once before heading south. The soldiers picked
1254 up the speed for a while but when the airplane
1255 did not return everyone slowed back down to
1256 a regular walking pace. Later, when the column

1257 had stopped for the night the sound of thunder
1258 crept into camp. A young boy was sent scurrying
1259 up a tall tree but could see no approaching storm.
1260 The mysterious noise kept growling for a time
1261 and then stopped abruptly. When he heard that, the

1262 Commander looked at his gathered sergeants and
1263 said simply, *They've found one of the other columns.*

CANTO XXVI

Whenever he stayed with his grandmother 1264
she would take him to the market. Everything 1265
you would ever want is there she said and to 1266
young eyes it was filled with wonder. There, 1267
old tires became shoes. Sheets of rusty metal scrounged 1268

from junkyards became shiny new pots and pans. 1269
Through the din of merchants hawking their wares, 1270
the craftsmen weave their spells, stooping over 1271
workbenches or hammering iron glowing orange 1272
from the roaring flames of the furnace. 1273

His favorite was the apothecary's shop. A 1274
place where folk magic came within reach. 1275
Pungent smells waited at the door as you 1276
entered. Bowls, boxes, bottles, plastic and 1277
burlap bags held nuts, withered frogs, roots, 1278

feathers, seeds, bones, dried fruits, and a 1279
rainbow of colored powders. Grandmother 1280
would roll out a list of ailments, both hers 1281
and various family members', and the apothecary 1282
would begin picking out the appropriate items. 1283

This fruit would handle most stomach ailments. 1284
That bark would stanch bleeding. Boil this vine 1285
for coughs, a tea of those leaves deadens pain, 1286
and use that resin as a plaster to heal any 1287
but the most severe injuries. 1288

Years later, when the war had begun,
he thought back to the apothecary shop and
wondered why no sorcerer had ever discovered
the spell or talisman that prevented one
tribe from envying another, that would

cure murderous hate. Perhaps
no magic was powerful enough for that.
We want what others have.
To take what they planted deep
in the soil and watered and watched over

through the relentless sun of the dry season.
To pull it out by the roots and eat it right there
and then as a thief in the night who
thinks of nothing beyond the next dawn
and the quick satisfaction of a full belly.

CANTO XXVII

Father Pierre found a small clearing 1304
off the track and set up for Mass with Lysette. 1305
He yearned to take her into the woods and 1306
confess the unholy terror and guilt 1307
that was clawing at him, a knife that 1308

swam through his bowels leaving him 1309
hollowed out of any of the joy he once 1310
felt when ministering to his flock back 1311
home. There, he imagined the faint smiles 1312
of the alabaster saints hovering along 1313

the walls, smiles of approval for 1314
his holy work in bringing the flock 1315
a few steps closer to their cold, distant love. 1316
Today, he was far from the church that 1317
had been his life, his purpose. The only 1318

Mass being said there now was the wind 1319
whispering through the shutters. The 1320
chorus was the buzz that hordes of blue- 1321
black flies made preparing for their next 1322
generation. Those statues he once looked 1323

on as old friends now wore tattered robes 1324
of dust and dark brown stains. Their 1325
faces grim as they kept watch over a 1326
silent congregation eternally waiting 1327
for his return. 1328

1329 Today he could only go through the motions
1330 of conducting the service for the living.
1331 His hands trembled as he offered consecrated
1332 hosts to warm pink mouths or laid them in
1333 palms rough from hard work. Could any

1334 of these, his new children, have been there
1335 that night? That night. That night.
1336 When all thought of God and Heaven,
1337 of his vows, his very soul, were thrown
1338 away, abandoned, sacrificed to the altar

1339 of fear and the desire to live at any cost.
1340 He could imagine the faces of those
1341 who had known, trusted him watching
1342 him run into the shadows of the woods
1343 just before being blinded by the headlights.

1344 When the service was over, he went down
1345 to a nearby stream to wash his hands and
1346 face to get rid of the bloody stains he feared
1347 were permanently imprinted in his flesh.

CANTO XXVIII

I do not like to fight. I did not want to be
in this war. Some of my friends from school
may be in the army chasing us. I've hated being
part of this madness since they took my cadet
class to the firing range near the base. As

soon as I stepped off the bus, bombs began
going off in my head along with a stabbing
pain that made me think I had been shot.
I could hardly hear the army officers
and sergeants yelling. The atmosphere

was electric, a pulsing sense of damnation
permeating every move despite the apparent
confidence of those in charge of our cause.
I could tell their fear of the Others underlay
their every gesture under that day's sun.

I was handed a gun, still slick with oil.
Well-machined steel and wood feeling solid.
Purposeful. Yet lighter than I expected.
It had a certain grace in its hard lines.
Determined to silence my doubts and the

thunder in my head, I tried to focus on
the lesson the instructor was yelling out.
Examining the gun. Learning how to handle
it. What the different parts were. Trigger.
Sights. Magazine. Bolt carrier. Even the

safety switch with its words Safe, Single Fire,
Automatic. The promise of white-hot
hellfire erupting from blue steel with only
the lightest pressure of my finger
needed to give it birth.

I did not want to be taught how to kill,
how to end a life in blood and pain.
Who are these men that expect me to start
breaking the Holy Commandments the priests
drilled into my head for so many years?

The war in my head really exploded when
I had to kneel at the sandbag wall
and aim the gun at the target.
The moment I could see the paper
figure clearly, the snarling face vanished

replaced by my mother's, then my
baby sister, my father. Even the
kindly woman who sold nuts
along the street near my house.
Later, at the hospital, I was told

that was when I started screaming…

—*Porter, 23*

CANTO XXIX

Claudine and Esther had just finished preparing 1395
their dinner of salted fish as darkness fell. 1396
She had just taken a bite when the sound of boots 1397
approached. She looked up in time to see the 1398
Commander pick his way through the crowd. 1399

Come join us Commander, she called. 1400
He recognized her, smiled, and came over. 1401
Don't mind if I do. It'll make a nice change 1402
from eating with the men. He sat down and 1403
accepted a fish and some spices from Esther. 1404

Besides, I've heard all their jokes, the Commander 1405
grinned, *Twice.* The women chuckle politely. 1406
Too bad this is all we have to offer, Esther offered. 1407
J'ai très faim. Besides, this is a feast compared 1408
to what many have, he replied nodding his head 1409

at clumps of people nearby who lay resting or 1410
sat motionless, some staring enviously at 1411
others who ate and drank just a few feet away. 1412
Some sharing went on but many held back, 1413
uncertain what was to come. *We just have* 1414

to make do until we reach the garrison where 1415
there will be fresh supplies and protection. 1416
We will be safe there and then you can cook 1417
me a fine meal. He leaned back against a large 1418
root and stared directly at Claudine who suddenly 1419

felt very shy. Still, they talked a little longer
as the darkness became nearly complete.
Finally, too soon, the Commander reached
into a pocket and brought out a flashlight.
I thank you for dinner, but an officer's duty

is never done. Please take care not to wander
far into the woods. I don't want to lose you
he said looking at Claudine. With that he was
off, the light walking over other groups of people
along the path. Claudine watched until it was

swallowed by the darkness and the sound of
his footsteps dove beneath the murmurings
of the people around them.

CANTO XXX

He was a hunter. He had never wanted to be 1433
anything else. There was no greater joy for 1434
him than when he put down his farm tools, 1435
picked up his bow and arrows and headed 1436
across his fields and into the forest. Since 1437

childhood he was always able to bring home 1438
meat when crops failed. His arrows found 1439
duikers, monkeys and, on rare occasion, wild hog. 1440
He knew where they lived, tracking their spoor 1441
deep into the woods beyond the last farms, 1442

climbing mountain slopes where cool breezes 1443
soothed and dried the sweat on his face. 1444
Further up, he followed trails into the clouds that 1445
descended to become the mists cupped in the 1446
bowls of ancient volcanoes. There the trees 1447

groaned under the weight of thousands of 1448
fruit bats gorged sticky from their feasting 1449
and iridescent birds who hovered as question 1450
marks in the whispering air. There he could walk 1451
in his ancestors' footsteps still holding on 1452

to the magic lost long ago in the lowlands 1453
where sacred trees were felled for firewood 1454
and tribal spirits drowned under cloying asphalt. 1455

1456	*The day the call came for everyone to do his or her duty,*
1457	*the milice gathered the townspeople in the square*
1458	*to relay instructions from the capital and give speeches*
1459	*to whip them into a frenzy. He declined*
1460	*the machetes of the maddened crowd, slipping*
1461	*instead into the forest with his trusted bow.*
1462	*Stalking dim trails on whisper-light feet.*
1463	*Leaving no discernable print in the mud*
1464	*to trumpet his passing to others who could*
1465	*still read the secret signs of the forest*
1466	*just as his father had taught him as a boy.*
1467	*Under a blue vault opening to dizzying eternity,*
1468	*he moved, poisoned arrow notched in the string,*
1469	*feathers smoothed back to part the air*
1470	*with a steadying grip so it would fly true.*
1471	*Heart pounding as it did at the start of every hunt.*
1472	*No greater thought than the pursuit and kill.*
1473	*Reciting a quiet prayer for success.*
1474	*At a place where he knew the upland farmers would*
1475	*pass on their way to market and their women*
1476	*to the river to fetch water, he waited making*
1477	*himself part of the lights and colors of the*
1478	*underbrush, bow and arrows at his side.*
1479	*There he sat through the hours while sunlit*
1480	*sky gave way to indigo night with stars so jumbled*
1481	*the constellations were lost in the confusion.*
1482	*Sometimes there would be movement nearby.*
1483	*Seeing each animal with his ears, he picked out*

a hoof gently pressing on a fallen leaf, fur
brushing fronds, even quiet snuffling as noses
strained to catch each smell brought by the wind
hunting for the one that might betray fang and claw.
He rested as the night wore on, closing his eyes,

back to tree trunk, comfortable for now
wondering how long before the crowd
from town flushed the families on the hillsides
above to flee their farms and homes down
into this valley. He tried not to think of the faces

of those he had hunted or shared meat with
who would be coming down the path to face
his arrows. He thought instead about his orders,
the warnings the radio shouted about plots
that had been discovered, bloody schemes foiled.

That survival would only, could only be assured
if every Patriot did his duty and squashed the bugs.
When he questioned his father, the old man
called the radio voices mad filth. The Hunter
shook his head. His father was wise but the

voices on the radio were from the Big Men
who had been to the world beyond the seas.
Surely they were wise too? Yet still he saw
in his mind the faces of old friends. His father's
friends. Laughing. Joking. How could they

have been hiding such foul plans all those years?
His head hurt with a hard concentration
that produced no good answers.

Toward morning, with the moon rising,
he finally heard a heavy rustling approach.
People. Breathing hard from their flight,
and fear. A child whimpering. Bare
feet thrumming on the dirt path. He

quietly removed the leather sheath from
a poisoned arrow and notched it. Carefully,
he then took up the tension on the bowstring.
The first dark figures passed by, bundles or
children balancing on heads or backs giving

them a distorted, monstrous look. He
waited as more passed. Then one figure
stopped in his line of sight. A man with his
back to the Hunter. He was motioning for
the others to hurry. Something about the man

made the Hunter lower the bow. After a few
more moments, the stream petered out.
The man then turned around and stared
straight into the dark brush at the Hunter.
For a moment, the moon illuminated his face

before he, too, was swallowed by the forest.
The Hunter re-sheathed his arrow, got up, and
silently began the long walk home. On the way
back he wondered if his mother had any idea
where Papa was tonight.

CANTO XXXI

Runihura's ego had been smarting since   1537
the Commander took away the woman.   1538
He was angry and humiliated about being   1539
faced down by a mere soldier. Him,   1540
a man of considerable responsibility   1541

in the government. Even the President's   1542
widow had praised him for his tireless   1543
work for their people. Now this *paysan*   1544
dared to give him orders? He flexed his   1545
powerful hands imagining the Commander's   1546

neck cracking between them. *Merde,*   1547
he still had needs. He got up and strode   1548
a short way up the path. His men knew   1549
what he wanted and kept a respectful distance   1550
so as not to become the object of his wrath.   1551

No regular soldiers were in sight. He   1552
looked around and saw a young couple trying   1553
to avoid his gaze. The wife was a nice piece   1554
he decided. He strode over and grabbed her.   1555
The husband started to object but was laid flat 1556

by a single blow from Runihura's massive fist. 1557
Then before the wife could start to scream, he 1558
clamped one hand over her mouth and dragged   1559
her into the bushes. His men laughed appreciatively 1560
as the sounds of a struggle slowly died away.   1561

Much later, Runihura emerged alone from the wall of leaves and vines, the darkness hiding the triumphant look on his face.

CANTO XXXII

In the dream it was late at night. 1565
I left the house my men had taken 1566
over to use as a base to sweep 1567
the surrounding hills during the war. 1568
I walked down a grassy slope and onto 1569

a pebbly beach on the lake shore 1570
where I once played as a child. 1571
Small waves lapped the mirrored stones 1572
while breezes set clusters of reeds 1573
swaying in a delicate, hypnotic dance. 1574

It seemed I stared for hours before realizing 1575
the reeds were actually arms held aloft 1576
in a mute appeal to the heavens. 1577
I sat down on the stones and watched 1578
the waters shimmer their broken reflections 1579

back to the stars drifting among the clouds 1580
wondering how many bodies lay hidden 1581
just beneath the surface welcoming 1582
curious fish with rigid stares and cold embraces. 1583
Their lips asking, asking beyond sound 1584

who should carry this stain on their hands. 1585
In answer, the moon peeked out from 1586
behind her silvery veil and stretched 1587
a single finger across the rippled lake 1588
towards the beach. No matter where 1589

I walked on the shore that night or any
night thereafter, it always pointed at me.

—Milice, 41

CANTO XXXIII

The sky was still in that colorless purgatory
between night and day when the soldiers
moved up and down the path waking people.
No time to prepare breakfast or steal a cold bite.

Hurry.

The enemy might be close and could attack at any time.
Leafy shadows could be hiding eyes of cold murder.
People stumbled along half asleep, parents carrying
children on backs already bent under large sacks.

Faster.

One man with a pulped face wandered the emptying
camp croaking a woman's name. Several bodies lay
unmoving where they fell asleep, souls fleeing far
beyond the reach of vengeance.

Keep going.

When the first rays of light began to slant among the
trees, the column was already far away. Later, during
their afternoon rest stop, they could hear the aircraft
again. Circling for nearly an hour to the south.

Be still.

A new kind of hunter tracking prey, the sky a conspirator
with metal wings. The Commander climbed a tree and
watched it fly low behind a nearby ridge, dropping large
black eggs, somersaulting, out of its cargo hold.

1617 *Don't look.*

1618 Now the air whistled in its new role, morphing from
1619 innocent bystander to assassin. A moment later, flames
1620 and smoke boiled out of the forest. Mission accomplished,
1621 the airplane flew over the column before heading east.

1622 *All clear.*

1623 Once it disappeared, the Commander barked new orders.
1624 By the time he had climbed back down to the ground,
1625 the column was on the move again.

CANTO XXXIV

As they walk through the narrow green 1626
tunnel, spiky leaves reach out to score blood. 1627
The female jungle is always fertile, 1628
always eager to offer a warm red embrace, 1629
her smile hidden behind veils of ferns 1630

and creeping vines. Her lovers lost 1631
in canopied mysteries. Their entreaties 1632
becoming the dry sound of the wind 1633
whistling through empty bones. 1634

CANTO XXXV

1635 Father Pierre was teaching the small girl
1636 on his shoulders how to recite the Hail Mary
1637 when the same thunder as the day before erupted
1638 again. This time it was nearer so there was no
1639 mistaking the sound of guns and grenades. The

1640 soldiers did not need to urge the tired refugees
1641 to move faster, people were nearly running now.
1642 Father Pierre kept the child on his shoulders
1643 while pulling her mother who was limping in pain.
1644 Ahead of him, Lysette was trying to help a trio of

1645 elderly matrons who, despite their fear, were
1646 falling farther and farther behind. As he caught
1647 up to her, he could see how the women
1648 were covered in sweat and close to collapse. On
1649 an impulse, he called to Lysette to help him.

1650 Turning to the women, he said he would be back
1651 soon to help them. They barely heard through
1652 their misery. He then had Lysette take the mother's
1653 other hand and together they half-dragged, half—
1654 carried the sobbing woman. As they turned a

1655 bend in the path, Father Pierre tried to not to feel
1656 the older women's eyes drilling into his back.
1657 Soon he could see those women would have
1658 plenty of company as more people fell out of
1659 line. A few soldiers stopped to pick up children.

Some men and women could be seen carrying older people. One boy even pushed an ancient man in a wheelbarrow. Many others, however, were left to fend for themselves. Father Pierre tried to say a little prayer for the soul of each

person they passed but soon was too focused on keeping his own feet moving.

CANTO XXXVI

The Sergeant was a big man, a brave warrior.
He fought well against the rebels
once killing four of them with his gun
then two more with his bare hands.
He did not swagger his victories

but spoke quietly of his farm and a
family trapped behind enemy lines
of whose fate he had no word.
After one mission the unit returned
to town exhausted and beaten from

their losses in the field. He disappeared
while the other survivors drank at
a local cabaret. Later, his friends
searched the town for hours
before finding him in a brothel

kneeling before an older woman.
His head cradled against her breasts,
a child crying for all he had lost
but with a strength that took the
rest of the team to pull him off.

–Soldier, 22

CANTO XXXVII

It was mid-afternoon before the Commander
called a halt. The column was now stretched
dangerously along the trail. Delaying now to
give the stragglers a chance to catch up galled
the Commander but everyone was worn out.

Also water was needed. Scouts found a stream
in the woods nearby. Soon a line of people
carrying jugs was snaking through the forest,
their thirst reeling them in towards the trickling
flow. Once there, they jostled for a space,

their feet churning the stream into thick mud.
Late arrivals had to walk farther into the forest
to find clean water. The soldiers tried to
maintain order but they, too, were tired
and thirsty. Soon many were helping
themselves to the refugees' water jugs.

CANTO XXXVIII

I think about my mother every day.
She would come to wake me with
the dawn's light wrapping her face
and hair in gold. She rarely talked
but her hands spoke soft loving words

as she helped me get ready for school.
Later, when I left my father's house to
join the other children heading down
into the valley, she would kiss me and
stand in the doorway, waving until I

was out of sight.

While my father taught me the things
every boy must know to become a man
within the tribe, my mother brought me
the purpling clouds and the first star of
the evening with dinner every night. Her

hand, touching my cheek, always left a
warm mark even after I had gone to bed.

—Refugee, 15

CANTO XXXIX

Claudine and Esther were early arrivals
at the assembly point so they had taken
care of their thirst and hunger before
many people had even arrived. They
were dozing in the shade when an aggrieved

voice asked *What, no lunch?* Claudine
blinked into the sun and saw the Commander
beaming at her. In his hand he had a water
jug. *I brought this thinking you might be too
tired to make the run to the stream but I see*

I am too late. He sat down next to Claudine
and chuckled at Esther's deep snoring.
Even though he was in better spirits Claudine
noticed how drawn his features were.
His uniform was covered with dust from the path.

They talked about their pasts. His in the army
and hers in a hospital, but by some unsaid rule,
stopped short of discussing anything to do with
the war. It was not long though, in the drowsy
heat of the afternoon and the exhaustion from

the march that Claudine's head dropped to rest
comfortably on his shoulder and his against her
head scarf. Neither spoke again. Soon
both were imitating Esther's snores.

CANTO XL

He dreamt that just before climbing down
behind the seared hills of ancient rock, the Sun
sent out his dimming searchlights across the underside
of his entourage of ragged clouds—a laying on of
hands to soothe the raw, red wounds opened that day.

His sister, the pale Moon with her entourage
of restless spirits tried the same trick hours later
but her cold fingers had no healing powers
leaving the faces of her children steeped in
funereal gray and eyes black as charcoal.

It wasn't until the thwarted Moon had, herself,
left in silent grief that the "Go" signal came.
Ghosts rose out of the dirt and roots out of the
forest to float silently against the breeze.
Down out of the bony hills they haunted game

trails and talus slopes. From its perch in a tree
above them, a leopard waited frozen and
unblinking for these gliding shapes to pass.
When the night was old and rumors of dawn
wafted among the stars, contact was made.

Lightning and thunder danced among the trees
while ricochets whined viciously in the night air.
Red flames flickered weakly and then died, drowning
among the wet leaves. In the lightening sky,
a hawk screamed his challenge to this intrusion.

As the sun's rays pierced the forest canopy, smoke   1772
drifted through the brush. Next to a silent gun,   1773
dark blood trickled slowly across a boulder,   1774
dripped into a rushing stream,   1775
and was gone.   1776

CANTO XLI

1777 Father Pierre was resting in a small gully
1778 with several families when something
1779 knocked hard against a nearby tree trunk.
1780 An instant later came the crack of the gun
1781 that fired it. A couple more followed tentatively

1782 and then the forest erupted. Everyone slipped
1783 deeper into the gully as leaves and wood chips
1784 rained down on them. Nearby, he could hear
1785 the guns from their own soldiers adding their
1786 voices to the fatal dance. Then grenades started

1787 exploding close by. Father Pierre knew they
1788 had to get out. He looked over at Lysette who
1789 was a few yards away cradling a whimpering
1790 toddler. He pointed down the length of the gully
1791 and she nodded agreement. They both then

1792 prodded the others into crawling in a single file.
1793 They got about 20 meters before they realized the
1794 gully was actually veering towards the approaching
1795 sound of their attackers' guns. Father Pierre wriggled
1796 his way close to the center of the group. *We must*

1797 *climb out and run. They will be here in moments.*
1798 *You know what will happen then.* He left that statement
1799 open knowing their fears would fill in the rest.
1800 The others nodded. Father Pierre did not hesitate.

1801 *Now* he shouted.

They clambered up the steep slope and burst out of the gully. Immediately two men near him were thrown onto their faces by the blast of a grenade. A few steps more and the woman whose child Lysette carried gave a short cry and crumpled. Everyone was moving fast, their fear

giving their feet wings. Even as Father Pierre called out for divine help, two more people fell. Suddenly, they were on the path. Everyone dove to the ground among the other refugees cowering under the intense gunfire. Moments later, Father Pierre realized with horror that

they were caught in a cross fire as the attack was coming from both sides of the path now. The soldiers at the end of the column could not help as they were trapped to his left. There was nothing here to stop this part of the column from being overrun.

He got up on his hands and knees and began urging those around him to follow him towards the column's head. *Anywhere but here* he shouted. Some began to follow him. He was relieved to see Lysette behind a tree with the child still clinging tightly. Their eyes met for a

moment and she, too, began to crawl.

CANTO XLII

While some of the milice rested,
others went into the bush looking
for something, anything to fill
their empty bellies. Those from
the cities followed their country

cousins closely. A bog was found
and some began digging into its banks.
Out of the mud emerged a large toad,
black and green on its warty back
with a poisonous yellow underbelly.

What scared the milice men was its
deep red mouth. One fighter wondered
if the toad was a vampire spirit gorged
fat on the spilt blood of their victims.

CANTO XLIII

The Commander woke with the bark of the first gunshot. 1837
He jumped to his feet when the enemy fullisade began. 1838
Looking down at Claudine who was now awake as well, 1839
he said *Stay here for now. If the shooting gets closer,* 1840
try to get to my men at the head of the column. 1841

If you can't, then just run in the opposite direction 1842
of the fighting. Impulsively, he said *I love you* then 1843
turned and ran towards the fighting without waiting 1844
for a reply. Claudine said quietly *I love you too* as 1845
she and a very awake Esther gathered their things. 1846

The Commander reached his reserve unit where the 1847
men had already thrown themselves into a cordon 1848
around the path. He sent a runner back up to the 1849
vanguard unit to send what they could spare. 1850
Peering intently into the forest, he could see 1851

distant movement heralding the impending assault. 1852
To the lead sergeant he said, *They are getting* 1853
Into position to attack all along the column. 1854
We won't be able to hold everywhere. They 1855
will cut us into little chunks. He bit his lip in 1856

concentration for a moment and then shouted, 1857
Everyone to me. Drawing his revolver, he 1858
launched himself into the woods. Soon he 1859
found a dry creek bed and ran down its length. 1860
When he had gone about 20 meters, 1861

he stopped and got his men into position.
We stop them here. We cannot let them surround the column. His men barely had time to form a firing line before the head of the enemy assault force appeared. Still thinking the column's

soldiers were strung out along the path, they ran heedlessly into the reserve force. Dozens died in the opening volley. Blood misting the trees as bullets tore uniforms and hurdled bodies

against those coming up behind them. The Commander went up and down the line shouting encouragement and firing his pistol to let his men know he was fighting too.

The storm was in full swing now. This was the chance many had sought. Here was the sum of all their fears—the sweaty terrors that gripped them day and night—now made flesh. Flesh that could

bleed. So his men poured precious ammunition into their pursuers with desperate abandon. Small trees between the two forces staggered and fell from the invisible chain saw. Bits of leaves and wood

splinters fell to coat the men. Their noses were
filled with the smell of cordite, sawdust, and blood.
The fire soon began to slacken when everyone's
ready clips were used up. Now men had to stop to
laboriously feed rounds into magazines.

A few went about it mechanically. Faces
set. Eyes with a faraway look. Numb
to the closeness of Death. Automatons.
Others found it more difficult. Rounds dropping
from shaking fingers. One man wept,

hardly able to move as the tree he hid
behind shuddered from bullets slamming
into the trunk. Again and again.
A snarling beast clawing maniacally at
the tree's flesh trying to reach him.

The Commander was shocked to see
Runihura in the line as well. He
gave the milice leader a brief nod but
Runihura only spared him a cold
glance before turning his attention

back to the battle. Once the enemy
got over their initial confusion, they
redoubled their efforts and with each
passing minute poured more troops into
the fight. The added weight to their

firepower began to tell. Around him,
the Commander could see men falling.
His troops' fire began to slacken
as fewer dared to raise their heads out
of the creek bed to face the sheets of

bullets slicing through the undergrowth.
He could see eyes darting to either side.
Here and there heads starting to turn slightly
scanning escape routes back into the forest
as panic began stirring under the roar of

the guns. He could feel the line wavering,
only minutes before it would break
completely in wild flight leaving the
civilians in the column unprotected.

Suddenly a new crash of gunfire opened
up as the forward unit hurled into the
enemy's unprotected flank. Panicked,
the enemy survivors broke and fled into
the forest. In moments they were gone.

Even as this battle suddenly ended, the
shooting nearer the path died away as well.
Some of the soldiers raised a ragged cheer
the Commander cut short as he barked orders.
Gather the wounded and as much ammunition

as can be carried and get back to the column.
Back on the path, there was little celebrating.
Towards what had been the rear of the column,
few people were still standing. The moaning
and crying drifted through the smoke-filled

forest. So many lay unmoving on the forest
floor surrounded by blood that it was
almost impossible to step on clean dirt.
The hum of flies was growing as they greedily
swarmed over the faces and wounds of the

fallen. Only a shadow of the rear guard
was still alive. Among the contorted
bodies, there were some lying savaged,
but still breathing. They had no doctor,
little medicine, and no time for treatment.

Every fibre of his body was screaming
they had to leave now before the enemy
regrouped and attacked again. Each
moment counted. Still, he could not just
leave them in their pain waiting for the

inevitable bitter end that awaited them.
Many eyes were staring at him with fear,
unspoken questions, or just resignation.
With a deep breath the Commander came
to a decision. He straightened himself

and in his best parade-ground voice began,
Soldiers, Cityoens. Through your bravery
today, we have won a great victory…
as he pushed a fresh magazine
into his pistol.

CANTO XLIV

1966
1967
1968
1969
1970

1971
1972
1973
1974
1975

1976
1977
1978
1979
1980

1981
1982
1983

1984

In my section there was this teacher
whose only possession was an old yearbook
from the school he taught at before
the war. At every rest stop he would
find a quiet place, open it and begin

methodically cataloging every face:
This one a student who loved the
existentialism of Sartre. That one
a star football player who
everyone said would one day play

on the national team. There is that
funny math teacher who loved to play
pranks on the stuffy school administrator.
After each name he would then list
their fates. Shot. Macheted. Burned alive.

People whispered that his chest was covered
in small scars, one for each name to help
him better remember their stories.

— *Soldier, 19*

CANTO XLV

Father Pierre was applying *antiseptique*
to an old man's wound while Lysette
was binding a boy's injured arm
when the shooting started again.
He nearly got up to run when

he realized the shooting was not
the chaotic stutter of guns on
full automatic but single shots
evenly spaced out.
It grew closer and soon he saw

the Commander leading a group of soldiers.
The priest saw they all seemed
to be searching for something among the bodies.
At random each would stop,
kneel for a few heartbeats,

then rise up, take aim with their weapon,
fire it at something on the ground,
and then move on.
When he reached Father Pierre,
the Commander stopped and

looked at him with haunted eyes.
A pistol in his hand that still
exhaled a wisp of smoke.
Is she gone? he said indicating
a woman lying next to Father Pierre.

2010 *Yes,* Father Pierre replied.
2011 *So many,* the Commander said
2012 looking at the gun as if seeing it
2013 for the first time, *so many, by my own hand.*
2014 Father Pierre could only sigh,

2015 *If they could not walk,*
2016 *they were dead already.*
2017 *We all know our fate if taken.*
2018 *Your bullet is the only mercy*
2019 *our wounded can expect.*

2020 *Please remember there are plenty*
2021 *of the living who still need you.*
2022 The Commander could only nod
2023 wordlessly before striding off.
2024 As he moved on, Father Pierre watched

2025 him go and thought to himself,
2026 *He will need a miracle to*
2027 *get us to that garrison and*
2028 *God doesn't seem very inclined*
2029 *to grant us any right now.*

2030 Father Pierre then began organizing
2031 the survivors close by to gather
2032 what food and water they could find
2033 before the soldiers gave the signal
2034 to move out.

CANTO XLVI

After so much war, all I want   2035
is to live by the sea. Not for the fish, crabs   2036
or whatever else the tide or fishermen   2037
throw onto the beach. Not for the dawns   2038
or sunsets where God paints the   2039

clouds with new colors invented just for   2040
that day, for you. Nor for the breezes   2041
that bring new smells that tell tales   2042
of faraway lands. No, I want the waves   2043
that slam and tear into the sand all night long.   2044

I want that noise to silence the ghosts in my head   2045
and the bright moon to chase them   2046
back into the shadows.   2047

—Gendarme, 33   2048

CANTO XLVII

2049 A short time later, the much-shrunken column
2050 was on the move again. The sun dipped into
2051 a solid bank of clouds. Hours passed but the
2052 soldiers kept urging everyone to keep going.
2053 Even when the clouds covered the sky and

2054 the heavens opened up with lightning and
2055 blinding sheets of rain they did not stop.
2056 When night fell and they could not see their
2057 hands in front of their faces, they kept going
2058 holding on to the person ahead of them. Only

2059 when the rain finally ended after midnight
2060 to reveal a crescent moon and people were
2061 stumbling with exhaustion was a halt
2062 finally called. Most collapsed where they
2063 stopped without making any attempt to lay

2064 out mats or blankets. They lay sodden and
2065 broken in the darkness, watched only by
2066 glowing eyes high in the trees.

CANTO XLVIII

We lost God during the killing season.
From city alleyways to shadowy paths
winding through mountain forests,
we willingly turned our faces from Him.
We were schoolchildren on holiday,

finally being away from the frowning
foreign priests and nuns who left as soon
as blood was spilled at their doorstep.
Churches were shuttered or filled with
our victims so that the stench drove us

further into Satan's welcoming embrace.
The blood drowned the psalms in our hearts,
turning the consecrated hosts we later tried
to receive into dust upon our tongues.

I knew we were damned the day we
found that group of survivors in a field.
Clothes worn ragged from running.
Exhausted from the chase and hunger,
they simply stopped to await their fate.

When we arrived they did not pray or plead
for their lives or even the smallest of mercies.
As one, they turned their eyes away to
something we could not see. Something
that held them quiet through our taunts,

2091	*kicks and finally, the bloody machetes.*
2092	*For them, we no longer existed.*
2093	*Their souls already looked beyond us*
2094	*only needing the kiss of our blades to*
2095	*free them, at last and forever, from the fear.*
2096	*Once they were gone, so too was our courage.*
2097	*We were as empty as their looted houses*
2098	*and their clothed husks hidden in the brush.*
2099	*Their eyes, filled with a light that we could*
2100	*not share, haunted our nights in dreams*
2101	*that no amount of beer could drown.*
2102	*During the day they crowd along the*
2103	*edges of our vision, flitting away each time*
2104	*we finally dredge up the nerve to face them.*
2105	*Leaving us to paw at our piles of loot,*
2106	*covering our despair with loud bluster*
2107	*as we seek to spill even more blood*
2108	*to fill our forsaken hearts.*
2109	*—Storekeeper, 45*

CANTO XLIX

In the morning, Claudine woke to find herself staring
face-to-face with a snake. It seemed puzzled by all
these large creatures in its territory. After satisfying
whatever curiosity it had about her, it slithered off into
the bush. Even as the snake disappeared she did not

move, just staring down the path watching the leaves
and vines glimmer in the first rays of the sun. Edges
extremely sharp and bright against the misty rays
reaching through the canopy. Each falling drop,
a nugget of light gold that added to the steady beat

from other drops as the trees shed last night's rain.
For this moment at least, it is largely silent, as if
the forest, its animals and the refugees still huddled
in the shadows were all collectively holding their breath.
She tried to get up but her feet were swollen

and painful so she stayed seated massaging them.
She didn't even notice Esther was gone until she
heard her footsteps coming down the path. Esther
put down the water jug she had been balancing on
her head. *I woke up early and decided to get some*

water for today's walk since we don't know if
we will be stopping again before we reach the
garrison tonight. Claudine looked up sharply,
You mean tomorrow. No, tonight. I passed by
as the Commander was briefing the soldiers

and he said we moved farther and faster than
he thought we would last night so we can make it.
Claudine lay back and suddenly felt like she
could breathe for the first time in days. Esther
was glad to have been able to give her friend

some good news. *A few days in the garrison
camp, lots of food and rest and maybe even a bath,
and you will be presentable again for your new boyfriend.*
Claudine smiled, *It's nice to have something to look
forward to for a change.*

CANTO L

She was hesitant, unsure of how she should   2145
feel with him. Her heart wanted to open wide and   2146
take him into its warm embrace but she could hear   2147
her mother's voice insisting he first be brought home   2148
for inspection over a bowl of spicy pepper soup   2149

while the elders gathered to debate if he came   2150
from an acceptable clan. An honorable people.   2151
But old traditions have been swept away and   2152
her village, her people are gone. Some day   2153
they would be reborn when the spirits decided   2154

to return, maybe even within her. Until then,   2155
she would have to find hope wherever she could   2156
clasping a lifeline no stronger than a spider web.   2157

CANTO LI

2158 Back near the ragged end of the column,
2159 Runihura woke up achingly tired
2160 but in a rare good mood.
2161 He and his men had fought well yesterday.
2162 Even some of the Commander's soldiers

2163 seemed impressed,
2164 enough to let him share some of their
2165 dwindling supply of palm wine
2166 after they stopped.
2167 One of the newly widowed women

2168 now shared his bed.
2169 Once safely in the new UN camp,
2170 he would deal with that
2171 scum-sucking Commander.
2172 Afterwards he would make sure

2173 word got around
2174 how he was the one who led
2175 the troops to victory
2176 personally killing 10, no,
2177 make that 20 of the enemy.

2178 That should secure him a
2179 comfortable position in the
2180 new Liberation Front being organized.
2181 Perhaps even in Logistics which
2182 would give him the opportunity

to travel to Europe where he
could line his pockets like a politician.
Almost giddy with the possibilities,
he slapped the rump of the woman
lying next to him and ordered her

to get him something to drink.

CANTO LII

2189 *No food on the route.*
2190 *A child sucks on an old*
2191 *chicken bone.*
2192 *No more sustenance than*
2193 *a pebble or twig.*

2194 *But the hint of something*
2195 *to feed on*
2196 *or even the memory of*
2197 *food once there is enough*
2198 *to keep one foot going in*

2199 *front of the other.*

CANTO LIII

Father Pierre stared at Lysette
as she slept with her arms around
the child she had rescued.
He was struck at how beautiful
the innocence of the moment was.

He accepted that God may turn
His face from a cowardly priest,
a psychopathic milice leader,
even an army officer who killed
to spare those already doomed.

Still, he could not see how He,
in all His infinite Mercy, could
condemn the innocents in the column
along with the guilty or the uncounted masses
back home who died in brutal agony,

for no other reason than the name
of the tribe on their identity cards.
He put his hands together to plead
Spare them from this horror.
He closed his eyes and kept praying

until a soft hand touched his.
The little girl Lysette had been carrying
was smiling up at him. Lysette
sitting nearby offered her own
saying, *Mon Pere, it will be OK.*

2225 *Maybe He gave us our miracle last night.*
2226 *You'll see. The storm hid us and now*
2227 *we are safe. He does love us after all*
2228 *and will forgive us for what we did.*

CANTO LIV

Once the war is over, we will go home   2229
was the lie the people kept repeating to   2230
give themselves comfort against the looming   2231
threat driving them beyond exhaustion.   2232
Some could not even bring themselves to   2233

look back along the path they had come.   2234
Back through the forest towards distant   2235
mountains. In their minds, a great gate,   2236
ponderous with dread, had already closed,   2237
shutting off their past and everything they   2238

once had or ever hoped to have. The new reality   2239
was that home had become a village emptied,   2240
destroyed, or filled with strangers with hard eyes.   2241
Where thirsty machetes wandered the nights   2242
and severed heads are left in doorways.   2243

A warning. A statement of cold fact spearing   2244
last hopes: you no longer have any claim to the   2245
land of your forefathers than to the clouds   2246
in the sky or the spirit mountains   2247
on the moon.   2248

CANTO LV

2249 Once again the column got moving.
2250 The forest was thinning out a little
2251 and several meadows opened up.
2252 Just before noon the meadows gave way
2253 to farm fields and small houses.

2254 The soldiers searched each one in turn
2255 but all were deserted.
2256 Some food was found still in the ground.
2257 Unripe as it was people devoured
2258 every morsel greedily.

2259 The hope that many felt earlier
2260 in the morning began to fade
2261 as the hours went by and
2262 not a living soul appeared.
2263 Several of the milice scouting

2264 further afield than the others
2265 found a house with several
2266 jugs of palm wine.
2267 They bought them back to
2268 Runihura who wanted to keep

2269 improving his stature by insisting
2270 both milice and soldiers share.
2271 Soon many of the rear guard were drunk.
2272 Some sang.
2273 Others wandered off to find food.

When none was found in any of
the farmsteads they passed,
one frustrated milice man lit a
match to set a thatch roof on fire.
Within minutes several more

were burning.
The Commander was at the head
of the column sharing some
favorite jokes with his
soldiers when a shout

made him turn around.
For a moment, he could only gape
at the line of dark smoke plumes
marking the column's progress,
before he quickly picked a small

team and led them back along the path.

CANTO LVI

2290 The path wound among the hills
2291 steep slopes crowding on either side.
2292 Their peaks hiding far horizons
2293 blocking the dawn and twilight
2294 leaving room only for the noon sun

2295 except where the tall grass reached
2296 overhead forcing the column through
2297 dark tunnels dug by migrating animals
2298 fleeing the grassland's furnace drought.
2299 When they emerged from one tunnel,

2300 a living darkness descended as swarms
2301 of countless butterflies landed on
2302 cloth, skin and hair. Gentle greetings
2303 were offered in each whisper-light touch
2304 and the tiniest of cooling breezes

2305 from their wings. Then, as quickly as
2306 they appeared, the wind shifted and
2307 they left. Beating their wings in a kaleidoscope
2308 farewell. On the ground, a few remained.
2309 Damaged or dead. To become prey

2310 for the ants that rushed in to devour
2311 the colors of the fallen, hungry to capture
2312 those shimmering fragments of the sky.

CANTO LVII

Runihura was happily urinating
into an abandoned cooking pot
when a sudden blow from
behind sent him crashing
into the side of a *tukul*.

Dazed from the blow,
he staggered slowly to his feet
to face the Commander who raged,
You idiot, you've announced
our presence to everyone

within 20 kilometers.
Runihura roared right back,
You sneaky little weasel.
Only a shit like you would
hit a man from behind.

I'll gut you like a fish for that.
With that Runihura launched
himself at the Commander
who easily sidestepped the charge,
bringing down the butt of his pistol

on the back of the large man's head.
Runihura staggered and fell.
The Commander looked up to see
four milice men aiming their
weapons at him.

In the sudden silence, the sound
of a dozen bolts being drawn back
by his own soldiers was as loud as thunder.
The milice men lowered their weapons.
Take this drunken swine and

any of his goons who care to join him
and tie them to the nearest trees.
Let the enemy have them,
said the Commander icily.
Runihura growled and tried to

get back on his feet only to find
himself staring straight at the barrel
of the Commander's gun.
Yesterday I shot 23 people who
were too wounded to walk.

Anyone of them was a far better person
than you, you arrogant bastard.
It is because of your crowd and
the hate and lies you fed us
that we are now running and

dying in a foreign country. Even
after we were beaten and barely
surviving in filthy refugee camps
in another country, you and the
politicians had to keep raiding,

keep killing. All you managed
to do was to goad them into
attacking us to finish this war once
and for all. Now they won't
ever stop until we are all dead.

The Commander holstered his gun.
I hope they roast you for dinner.
He hit the big man again and again.
It hardly seemed to faze him.
Runihura spat out a tooth and

bloody saliva. *Don't think*
for a moment that you are
a good man. He looked around
the circle of faces. *Any of you.*
You could have sat this war out

or gone over the border but you stayed.
You knew damn well what was happening.
Don't cry for your virginity now.
He chuckled. *If we had only a little*
more time we could have finished those

cockroaches off for good. Then we
would have all been safe…
The Commander swung his boot
viciously into the man's groin.
Runihura collapsed with a

groan into a fetal ball.
The Commander shouted,
While you were showing
what a man you are
by slaughtering the defenseless,

my men were fighting and dying
to hold back the rebels.
Your great plan has turned to shit.
Now we are the ones that are going
to get slaughtered and the world

will thank those people out there for doing it.
He looked at the milice men,
Unless you want to join this vermin,
tie him up to the nearest tree.
We need to get back to the column.

CANTO LVIII

The politicians who shouted for blood   2403
are all gone now. Their shrill call to arms   2404
still echoes in our ears along with   2405
the humming that never left us   2406
from the constant gunfire.   2407

A few died with us on paths beaten into   2408
concrete under countless feet of our   2409
dwindling tribe. Many—most—left us for   2410
other shores. With passage bought on rickety   2411
Russian airplanes with looted cash for themselves   2412

and their piggish women, they abandoned us   2413
to empty promises of help as the dust   2414
kicked up by the propellers   2415
lay thick in our throats.   2416

CANTO LIX

As the Commander hurried back to the head
of the column, people started shouting and
pointing up in the sky. The plane had returned.
Run he shouted and the column melted as people
scattered in every direction. It didn't circle but

dove directly towards them. The Commander and a few
soldiers stayed on the path firing their guns trying
to drive it off or at least aim for it. Instead it
veered slightly and black shapes began falling out
of the rear hatch. Tumbling, they headed for the

tree line where many people were now hiding.
The Commander yelled as if his voice alone could
somehow deflect their paths but an instant later a
series of eruptions clawed through the trees sending
dirt and flames rocketing in every direction.

Heedless of the threat of shrapnel, the Commander
ran towards the explosions. He hadn't seen which
side of the column Claudine was on.
Oh God, let her not be in there he cried.
In moments he was among what was left of the forest.

Much that was once living there was now shredded—
whether it was made of hard wood or soft flesh.
Pieces of brightly colored cloth hung on tree branches.
Gaudy replacements for the leaves they once wore.
He staggered back out into the meadow to see hundreds

of people appearing out of the grass and the forest.
He shouted orders to soldiers and civilians alike to
search for survivors. On the path he looked desperately
for Claudine among the milling crowd. Minutes later
he saw her being led out of the forest by Esther.

Her dress was ripped and covered in blood.
He ran to her afraid she was now among the
seriously wounded. When he got closer and she saw him,
she ran towards him tearing herself from the grip of those
holding her. Moments later they flew into each other's arms.

He almost shouted, *Are you hurt?*
No she sobbed *the blood…it's not mine.*
He held on as if he could never let her go again.

CANTO LX

*At the university, the Student read
many books by poets from around
the world. He fell in love with the
American Robinson Jeffers saying to
anyone who would listen that*

*he was the only Westerner
who really understood the fierce
independence of the predator.
The disdainful look of a hawk's pride,
the regal one of a lion or the hungered*

*insanity of the hyena's. You know
what is exactly on their minds,
they give no pity, ask for none.
For when they kill it is only when
necessary for food or to defend family.*

*He said they are so unlike men who
revel in such honorable traits as cruelty
and deception. Perfecting betrayal, refining
greed. Using weapons that cannot distinguish
between victim or aggressor. Killing others*

*for vacuous ideals, savaging the innocent
just for fun. Now he lay shaded under a tree,
his cheek wet with a cooling tear. His still lips
parted in a new poem of tiny breaths over a
tongue where unsaid words lay bunched.*

Silence flowed through his body in waves that curled 2480
and lapped against the body's great red tabernacles— 2481
a weakening heart and flooded lung—while his 2482
soul peered out through the gaping hole in 2483
his chest at a cold new world. 2484

CANTO LXI

2485 Finally they found all the survivors
2486 who could walk, dealt with those
2487 who could not, and resumed the march.
2488 The Commander consulted a map
2489 outside a deserted village and

2490 ordered a change of course.
2491 The column, a ponderous snake,
2492 turned onto a new track.
2493 He explained to Claudine
2494 and his sergeants that he was sure

2495 the enemy knew by now they were
2496 heading for the garrison.
2497 He hoped the enemy would try
2498 to intercept them on the direct route
2499 they had been using

2500 so he planned to go around.
2501 If the column could slip by
2502 unseen it might buy them
2503 enough time to get the refugees
2504 across the river before their

2505 pursuers could react.
2506 Speed was of the essence
2507 but many were at the ends of their ropes.
2508 He had word passed down the line
2509 that anyone who could not keep up

should move deep into the forest to hide.
If they were able to resume the march,
they should go west but stay off the path.
As his instructions were relayed, dozens
left the column and disappeared

into the undergrowth. Claudine saw
this and asked, *maybe we all should hide?*
The Commander shook his head.
They will sweep this area when
they realize we changed course.

A few people can safely hide.
Hundreds cannot.

CANTO LXII

An old man wept beside the path.
The woman stopped and knelt beside him.
Are you hurt? she asked.
No, these tears are for my farm.
My crops will be ready to harvest now

but my sons died in the war and I lost
my wife to disease in the camp. My father,
grandfather and every ancestor I was ever
told of farmed that land and now I will die
too far away for my spirit to find its way

back home to join my forefathers.
Everyone I ever knew is either dead or
running like us. My farm, our village
has become the inheritance of bitter ghosts.
Soon the forest will swallow it up as we

are being swallowed in this one. It will
be like we never existed. Because of
what I did—what we all did—our line
is broken, never to be repaired. No
one will come after. No one will

tend the shrines or make the sacrifices.
Then what will happen? He went
back to sobbing. She had no answers
for him. No comfort. So she left without
another word and stumbled back

into the column to hide.

CANTO LXIII

As the sun settled in the hills,　　2548
they reached a treeless ridge.　　2549
From there they could look　　2550
across the valley to the river　　2551
they had to cross to live.　　2552

A halt was called for the night.　　2553
Scouts were sent on ahead to see　　2554
what might be waiting for them.　　2555
Father Pierre stretched out on the grass,　　2556
Lysette and the child next to him.　　2557

Of the dozens whom he had started　　2558
the journey with, only three others remained.　　2559
As the sun sank out of sight, he stood　　2560
on aching feet and began the Mass alone　　2561
since none of his usual servers had survived.　　2562

Then as if a hidden door opened somewhere　　2563
his shrunken flock began to swell as　　2564
dozens then hundreds drifted in　　2565
to kneel in front of him. As he sang　　2566
the litanies, his voice joined　　2567

others in a swelling chorus which　　2568
carried across the bowed heads and　　2569
into the air over the misting valley.　　2570
His eyes fell on the Commander, Claudine,　　2571
and the soldiers as they, too, kneeled.　　2572

He tilted his head back and looked to
the first stars in the darkening sky and
prayed, *Oh Lord of Love and Mercy,
please don't abandon us now.*

CANTO LXIV

The dim forest was speared by 2577
the slanted pillars of sharp sunlight 2578
when she crossed one, its pressing heat 2579
felt almost solid and the cool darkness 2580
just beyond a relief as real as a splash 2581

of water on her head after a race. For 2582
a race was what she was in now. She hadn't 2583
heard from her pursuers in a while but she 2584
doubted they had given up the chase. Trying 2585
not to make much noise but she could not 2586

help the snapping twigs under her feet and the 2587
slaps of leaves she flew past. Even the 2588
backpack flailing from side to side did not help. 2589
She had debated just dropping it but losing 2590
the contents would have been just too much 2591

to bear. Not just the food and little water that was 2592
left but other things she could not bear to part 2593
with. Normally, its weight would barely have 2594
registered but now each ounce was a stone 2595
dragging her down, straining legs that were 2596

liquefying in the dead air of the forest. It was not 2597
long before her fear could no longer compel 2598
muscles to work like they had months ago on 2599
the school track. Her lungs clawed for air as 2600
fireflies danced in her eyes. Poor diet and disease 2601

*had robbed her athlete's strength. Cramps. Tremors.
Finally, she just slowed to a stop and with her last reserves
staggered off the track, dropped to her knees, and
crawled into the underbrush. Everything was shutting
down. She collapsed into a heap as sleep blotted out*

*the hunger and the pain. As her eyes closed, she felt
herself falling, falling far into the welcoming darkness.
Her face, if she could have seen it, changed as it threw off the
grief of this world. Lines faded. The tight set of her jaw
relaxed and once more she was the young girl she once was.*

*She was home again. It was afternoon falling away.
The weakening sun was giving the nomadic clouds
above a rosy hue. She stepped from the crowded
bus to jog up the street to her house. The city
was settling into its evening cacophony when she*

*ran through her front door. Inside, her backpack
flew off as she bounded into the kitchen
expecting to see her mother at the stove and
smell a savory stew. But there was
no dinner. Mama was sitting at the table.*

*A tin box—the one she kept old family photos in—
lay empty in front of her. Beyond her, people filled
the room. Translucent. Furnishings behind them
dimly seen. She knew instantly they were only the
afterthought of the light. Memories trying to cast*

new shadows. Eyes looking from empty mirrors.
They were men and women in outfits she had only seen
in history books standing quietly. While she recognized
what they were, she was not afraid for they were all
smiling at her. Mama was smiling too as she rose and

reached for her hand. Instead of the warm touch she
expected, there was only a cool breeze crossing her
skin. Even though they stood next to each other, she
could not see Mama clearly as her face seemed to jump
in and out of focus. The girl had questions but

a new sound approached. Rattling beads. Rustling fabric.
Chanting voices so low they were felt more than heard.
The crowd parted and a tall woman with piercing eyes
approached her. Hair cascading in waves while two large
snakes coiled themselves around her arms. Inhabitant

and ruler of the rivers and oceans of her mother's homeland.
By turns generous and cruel. Devourer of the unfaithful.
Recipient of Mama's devotions despite Papa's efforts
to convert her to the pale Christian god. The silent icons
he had hung on the walls could only watch as this fierce

deity crossed the room and stood before the girl. The
murmurings stopped. The girl felt a great presence
brush against her mind. Then in words that seemed
to form inside her own head, the goddess spoke:
Your mother's family have long served me. When

others failed me or turned to other gods, they stayed true. Now the spirits of your people have prayed for me to protect you in this dark time. I will grant their wish. If you need my help just call and I will answer. Before the girl could think of what to say, hands grabbed her suddenly from behind and spun her around. There was Papa covered in bloody wounds gripping her by the shoulders yelling Wake up now. And she did. Once again she was assaulted by the agonies of the real world. What was different was a rhythmic thrashing in the background growing steadily louder. After several minutes she realized it was people beating the underbrush with sticks. The enemy was closing in. Still exhausted, she got painfully to her feet and began hobbling deeper into the forest as reality's madness rediscovered its name.

To travel beyond the demands of her failing body, she tried remembering the joys of her life before but no memories presented themselves. Try as she might, her world had shrunk to this forest. This nightmare. Her terror underlined by the voices she could hear shouting and laughing as they confidently closed in on their quarry. She closed her eyes and began praying for rescue. At first, nothing happened. Then the pain in her legs began to ease. Still, the sounds of her pursuers grew until suddenly, a soldier stepped out of the bushes ahead of her. He looked neither left nor right but marched unseeing past her. More walked right *by but none acknowledged her presence. Ahead, she saw a lighter area that indicated a break in the forest's gloom. Her strength continued to ebb and she had to clutch at branches and hanging vines for support. Only when she felt ready to give up did she break out into a clearing. Filling much of the open space was a small river bounded by tall reeds. The only direct path to the water was a large flat boulder that jutted out into the water as a natural pier. With the last reserves of strength, she staggered to the rock and collapsed where it overhung a deep pool. Sobbing and eyes closed tight, she desperately prayed to the goddess for help as the shouts and whistles went on all around her. A gunshot went off and she looked around. Still, no one in sight. A glint caught her eye and looking into the water she saw an enormous carp hovering just under the surface. Iridescent in the dark water it transfixed her with eyes more piercing than any fish. Once again a great force brushed against her mind.*

Images of another world were shown and a promise offered. The girl nodded solemnly. She opened her backpack, removed the tin box and scattered the old photos her mother had treasured for so long. Then she began unbuttoning her shirt…

A short time later, several soldiers emerged from the trees. They found a small pile of ragged, dirty clothes, a backpack, an empty tin box and scattered pieces of blank photographic paper. A splash caught their attention and they saw the fins of two large fish sidle upstream. One soldier raised his gun but another, older man stopped him. He said something in their tribal dialect to the younger man then turned to where the water was still being ruffled by the fishes' passage and shouted Adieu, Madame Poisson. Nous respecterons votre décision!

CANTO LXV

After the service the Commander and
Claudine picked up a couple of water jugs
as they headed towards a nearby stream.
Under the dark trees, he took her hand
as they walked, his fingers sliding easily

between hers, the sensation making his
knees suddenly feel weak and his mouth dry.
When they reached the stream with its
mercury waters tinted with the deep scent
of unknown flowers hanging from vines

above them, they stopped on a small beach
and turned as one to suddenly embrace
as easily as if this was what had always
been planned. He bent his head to meet
hers for a kiss that started delicately then

was lost in their hunger.

After a minute, she pushed him back and
stepped into the stream and waded out
to a pool of somewhat deeper water.
She took off her dress and began to wash
herself. He watched her for a few heartbeats

outlined under the moon before he stripped
off his uniform and joined her.
The sounds they made were lost in the
rustle of the wind sliding through the trees.
Only much later did they return to camp.

Esther smiled as they passed by arm in arm.

CANTO LXVI

The boy climbed the tallest tree on the hill
until he broke through the upper reaches
of the leafy canopy to look out at the world.
The river valley and distant hills lay at his feet.
Settling in a notch formed by several branches,

he watched the setting sun burn the clouds
with its fire and pour gilt on their crowns.
The people below were miles away,
their voices caught, muffled in the leaves
and vines below him. So he stayed. Stayed until

the sun's fires on the clouds had burned themselves
out. Stayed until the gilt had worn off the edges.
Stayed until the clouds had become a gray tide
that billowed up drowning the last bright colors

leaving a paling afterglow in the fathomless sky.
Only then, with all the color drained away did the
sharp light of the first star break through.

CANTO LXVII

Just before dawn, the scouts returned.
The news was not good. Enemy forces
were blocking every approach to the
main highway bridge leading to the
besieged garrison. Even if the column

managed to cross the bridge, it would
have to fight its way through the besiegers
while their pursuers pounced from behind.
Even though the town's defenders were
holding, there was no way they could slip past.

Still, there was a ray of hope. The scouts
reported that a local told them that there was
an abandoned railroad bridge downstream
that the enemy had left unguarded. Every
heart in earshot leapt with unfamiliar

hope at the news. The scouts confirmed
that once across, they could go almost
anywhere in the rest of the province with
many towns and vast forests to lose
themselves in. But not for long.

The local said he heard the enemy
soldiers talking about more units on their
way to close that route as well. Hundreds
would arrive soon to bar the last crossing
leaving the column with nowhere to go

and their backs against the river…

2777 The Commander didn't hesitate.
2778 *We make for the bridge.*

CANTO LXVIII

In the dream, he clung desperately to the cliff 2779
with his hands and feet, his body pressed 2780
against the wet rock. Water from the falls 2781
sprayed in his eyes, blurring his vision. 2782
When he looked down, he saw the rock face 2783

was pockmarked with holes that were empty 2784
eye sockets. He knew every one of them was 2785
watching him. Yearning for him to fall... 2786

CANTO LXIX

2787 Orders were relayed across the camp
2788 and within minutes, people started
2789 moving downhill into the valley.
2790 Claudine and Esther had just
2791 shouldered their packs when

2792 Esther stumbled and cried out.
2793 Claudine and one of the older sergeants
2794 rushed to her side as she clutched at her leg.
2795 He knelt down, and after a quick examination,
2796 declared nothing was broken but her ankle

2797 was sprained. Esther stood up but nearly
2798 collapsed when she tried putting any
2799 weight on the injured leg. The Commander
2800 walked up and glanced at Claudine.
2801 An unspoken question passed between them.

2802 Esther and the sergeant saw it as well.
2803 Before the Commander could say anything,
2804 the sergeant spoke up, I will help her.
2805 With that, he put one arm around her and
2806 lifted to take the weight off her injured foot.

2807 The Commander picked up her pack and set off.
2808 Esther and the sergeant got going slowly
2809 with Claudine walking just behind.

The way down into the valley was steep
at first but soon began to ease into a gentle slope
before leveling out as they reached the valley floor.
After a couple of hours, Esther's face was paler
and shone with sweat. Still, she

kept going with the sergeant offering occasional
words of encouragement. The going was
difficult for her because they had to wind
among the primeval trees with large roots
that snaked across the path. At one point,

where the roots were thickest, the sergeant
suddenly swept Esther up into his arms and
carried her clear as if she was just a small child.
Peering over his shoulder, Esther caught
Claudine's eye and, despite her pain,

managed to give Claudine a wan smile.

CANTO LXX

The river's birth waters seep out of the mossy rocks
high in the mountains above the mist. Silent springs
beginning the long noisy run down through the jungle,
on into the ocean. Along the way they slow. Widening.
Meandering. Grazing at their restraining banks.

A cannibal river, it feeds on other springs and creeks
until it reaches the edge of the escarpment to
disappear over misty falls down into invisible gorges
under the shadows of ancient trees. Finally come the
great cataracts whose roar drowns the eagle's cry.

Beyond the cataracts, the waters slow again
as they rest from their headlong rush. Now gentled
in their broad bed, the last ripples die choked among
drifting meadows of water lilies and reedy islands.
Hidden among the green stalks, reptilian eyes keep watch.

On shore, the air is stifling even under the shadow
of the great green canopy. Syrup-thick to the
point that breathing is labored to extract
enough oxygen to feed worn muscles. The
trees crowd in closer as they approach a swamp.

Stumbling along, few in the column notice,
among the giants rising out of stagnant pools,
a silvery tree hanging suspended in a web
of thick vines. Amputated from the earth that
gave it life, this ancient victim of a thunderbolt

is firmly bound in their tight green embrace. 2851
Their leaves and flowers giving it the illusion 2852
of bountiful life. Now it is home to dreams 2853
and visions that wander with the night spirits 2854
to soothe, inspire, or terrify sleeping souls 2855

according to their magical formulae. In deference 2856
to its power over them, bowls of foods and 2857
palm wine, left as offerings by local villagers, 2858
lie scattered along the shore. Little caring for 2859
the appetites of local deities, those bowls were 2860

quickly emptied by people in the column 2861
to fill some very real bellies. 2862

CANTO LXXI

Having reached the river by late morning,
they turned north, crossing the edge of a swamp
just to the east of the river bank and staying well
within the shadows, away from prying eyes.
Soon they came upon a small village. Abandoned.

The arrival of grim soldiers upstream had been
broadcast through the bush telegraph. Guns
coming to kill. The locals did not wait to find
out who the targets were. Here, you get out
of the way until the guns leave. A rest stop

was called. Some food was found in the
village and distributed to those in greatest
need. Word passed quickly that the bridge
was close. The Commander went ahead
with a small squad to scout the approach.

A bird cry sounded in the trees. This was
the warning call from the soldiers—someone
was coming. Those out in the open ran
back into the shelter of the trees. Everyone
in the forest lay on the ground or crouched

behind something. Not a cough or a whisper
could be heard. On the river, a dugout canoe
appeared. *So not every local fled*, thought Claudine.
In the stern, a young man carved the sidling
waves with a broad-tipped oar while in the

bow, an older man with powerful arms whirled
weights which blossomed in flight into a large
net that vanished into the water. The older
man quickly hauled the net back in, flicked
a few silver fish into a basket, then got

ready to set the net again as the canoe
swung out of sight downstream. The
refugees watched with eyes hungry for
the normalcy of the moment they feared
was closed to them forever.

CANTO LXXII

The map was an old one, tattered by the years
and many hands. It showed the world as the
foreign colonialists once knew it. On the paper,
names they imported stood proudly over rivers,
mountains and towns denying whatever words

the locals used. The bridge the outsiders built
with iron forged half a world away still stood above
the flowing waters slowly dripping rust into
the busy current and eventually back into the earth.
The last time the rails vibrated with the passage

of the great iron wheels, the older officers
in the column were just children.

On the map, the railroad stretched west until
it fell off the paper. Far beyond where the guns
could go. This was their salvation. At least
on paper. As they studied the bridge from
the underbrush, however, they could see

that the old iron rails now lay hidden under
the roots of the ever-hungry forest.

CANTO LXXIII

The Commander returned and ordered the column to move out.
Word came down the line that once they crossed the river and
were safely past the enemy's cordon, the column would break up,
dispersing into smaller groups that could head for different towns
or continue west to some of the big refugee camps.

The rest seemed to have helped Esther. She was looking
better and was talking easily with the sergeant who
massaged her ankle. Once the word came to move out,
he helped her up and they set out with the steady pace they
had developed earlier. Claudine was talking with some

of the soldiers' wives when the Commander finished
consulting with his sergeants. He came over to where
she was. They embraced for a long moment before
gathering their packs and leading the forward unit
out onto the path.

Father Pierre offered prayers for an old woman
who had quietly passed away during the rest stop.
Since there was no time and no one had the energy,
they did not dig a grave but simply covered her
with leaves and palm fronds.

Lysette picked up the orphaned toddler and gathered
the group together (which had grown again since last
night's service) for a quick benediction from Father Pierre.
They then took their places in the column flowing quietly
into the deeper shade beyond the village's edge.

CANTO LXXIV

That morning Claudine and the Commander
stole a few moments to sit quietly
on a large boulder that jutted at an
angle as if rammed into the earth
by a mad giant or vengeful god.

Claudine looked at him as if for the first
time. A strange fluttering grew in
her chest as if she was about to unfold
wings and leap into the sky. For a
moment she could not recognize the

feeling. Then it hit her. She was happy.
How odd that just being able to sit and
relax with a man she was falling in love
with would feel so alien now after
so much pain and chaos.

An eagle flew over. The Commander's eyes
were closed so she put her hand on his
shoulder to get his attention. She could
feel his taut muscles through the worn
cloth. He opened his eyes and looked directly

at her. There was something in his gaze
that seemed to need answering but
she did not know the question. Before she
could think of something to say, two of
the scouts strode up and pulled

his attention away from her.

CANTO LXXV

The bridge. They could see it now
from the banks of the river as they approached.
Just as a palpable sense of relief was starting
to build—the end of a long race in sight—
a soldier ran up breathlessly with word

from the rear guard. They could hear the sound
of many, many feet approaching from behind. The
Commander swore. A trap was swinging shut. He
picked a squad and ordered them to guide the head
of the column across the bridge.

Keep everyone moving he said *once on the other
side tell the civilians to keep heading west or north.
Disperse if they can. Go!* He led the main body
of his men towards the railroad grade to meet the
expected line of attack. The front of the column

reached the bridge and began scrambling along
the rusted platform towards the far side. The Commander
stopped on the track bed with Claudine and the others.
While he barked orders to his soldiers to deploy,
she watched as the mass of people poured

across the bridge. Claudine was silently egging them
on—*faster, go faster*—as if they were sprinters nearing
the finish line.

Suddenly, a sharp roar of weapons on full automatic smote her ears. The Commander turned just in time to see a dozen enemy soldiers emerge from the thick undergrowth on the far side of the bridge, some almost invisible behind the jetting flames. The front ranks of refugees melted as the bullets slammed home. Road dust billowed as bullets sliced through clothes searching for flesh and bone. A low moan of agony was torn from hundreds of throats. Whether from desperation or the force of so many people pushing from behind, some people began dropping off the side of the ridge, falling into the river below. Within moments, however, somehow the incredible momentum of the crowd stopped and reversed itself as hundreds now frantically sought to escape the bullets scything among them. As the refugees scattered back into the forest they had just come from, the column's own soldiers could now return fire, killing several of the enemy and driving the rest back under cover.

The Commander quickly sent word for all soldiers to come up immediately to join him. The civilians still pouring into the area were directed to move into the forest just behind the railroad embankment. Hundreds of eyes watched the Commander and the soldiers anxiously.

Father Pierre, chest heaving, leaned against a tree. Two parishioners began reciting Our Father while Lysette, sitting close by, sang quietly to the little girl cradled in her lap. When enough of the soldiers were assembled, the Commander said, *They think they have us in a trap but I believe there*

are only a few of their soldiers facing us on the bridge. Now that we have pretty much everyone who can pull a trigger or throw a grenade, we need to attack. We have to force our way across regardless of the cost. Once the bridge is open and everyone is on that side, we will have to hold off our pursuers long enough to give our people a chance to disperse. Since this is still government territory, I don't think they will chase us much farther but the civilians shouldn't stick around to find out.
He looked around—at Claudine, the assembled soldiers and the many anxious faces of refugees within earshot.

We have all struggled so hard to get this far and have lost so much. Their lives, he said waving his hand indicating the refugees huddling behind the embankment and in the forest, *All of our lives, rest with you. We cannot fail. Bonne chance, mes amis.*

He pulled out his pistol. He kissed Claudine. *Ready? Let's go…*

CANTO LXXVI

Sometime later, a foreign journalist arrived
at the village looking for answers about what
happened to the last of the great columns of
refugees to disappear without a trace in that war.
Locals told of hearing a great battle at

the bridge from their hiding places in the forest,
with gunfire and explosions that rattled the trees.
For days afterwards there were other noises the
locals closed their ears to as troops hunted
for survivors in the woods and along the river.

When the soldiers were done, bulldozers and
flamethrowers were used to hide the evidence.
The burnings went on for days leaving a fine
gray ash covering everything for miles until
the next rainy season washed it away…

When asked whether any refugees survived,
the locals shrugged saying there were new
faces in villages and camps across the province.
People with unusual accents who could have
fled any one of a number of wars beyond

distant hills where militias fought each other
for power, for tribal pride, or for the riches
hidden in soil baptized with innocent blood.
Out west, beyond the reach of psychotic guns,
some drifted into towns hoping to hide quietly

among new neighbors, to reclaim lives, to heal wounds no one could see. Those whose pain was the greatest moved deeper into the forests to escape the world entirely with only the bonobo and okapi for company.

EPILOGUE

Etienne walked home that evening whistling.
Today was payday at the lumberyard and it felt
good to have a wad of money filling his pocket.
It was enough to buy food and some needed supplies
like the material his wife wanted to sew a uniform

for their child for when the schoolhouse
being built nearby was finished and the new
teacher arrived from the city. He might even be
able to save a few francs towards buying Henri's
old scooter to make the trip to town a lot easier.

The road he followed still seemed new even after nearly
three years. He had had to move after the fires died.
The forest he had lived in all his life was slashed
with new clearings ringed with burnt tree trunks and
carpeted with freshly turned earth. Even during the

day, he could hear dry whispers filling the shadows,
empty of substance and yet full of regret. Yearning for
a forgiveness that would never come. Even as the brush
and flowers crept in to hide the scars, he could not stay
in such a haunted, violated place so he bundled up his

new family and moved miles downriver to make a
home where the trees were at peace.

At last, he reached his house. He looked with satisfaction
at the patch of ground that was cleared for planting
and the newly completed corral of branches and vines
to keep their chickens from wandering into the road.
He walked through the open doorway and saw his wife

stirring a pot over a fire. As his shadow fell on her,
Lysette turned and smiled. He laughed as she stood
and came into his arms. They kissed only for a moment
before a little girl ran giggling in from the backyard
throwing her happy weight against his legs.

POSTSCRIPT

Back east that year, an early rain came to the
hills heralding the approach of the monsoon
season. When it had passed, a herd of deer emerged
from the dripping forest to stand hesitantly at the edge
of the field. For months they had been driven off their

usual grazing range by the rumbling, cracking earth,
the shuddering trees and the bitter reek of
the angry clouds billowing from the peaks above.

Now, finally, the rocks are quiet, a new wind freshens the
air and the grass, which had grown tall, is sweet.

ABOUT THE AUTHOR

Andreas Morgner has worked for the U.S. Department of the Treasury as an investigator since 2001. Between 2008 and 2011, he was assigned to the U.S. Africa Command (AFRICOM), a military command based in Stuttgart, Germany. During that time, he traveled extensively in Africa investigating war crimes as well as drugs and arms smuggling. It was also during that period that he began gathering the material that became *KINYAMASWA*, his fourth collection of poetry. His third collection, *When You Come Again, You Will Never Go* won Unlikely Books' 2009 poetry competition; in the same year, a poem from that collection won *Consequence Magazine's* annual poetry award.

Several of the cantos in *KINYAMASWA* were submitted as stand-alone poems to writing competitions in the US and UK in 2013. These of which won or placed in the following contests: The Dorothy Sutton Award (1st Place), The Hespeler Memorial Award (3rd Place), Aquillrelle (Finalist), Southeastern Minnesota Poets Award (Award of Merit), Helen Pappas Memorial Award (Citation), and the Pendle War Poetry Competition (in the UK) (Special Merit Award).

Morgner lives with his family near Washington, D.C.

Apprentice House Press
Loyola University Maryland

Apprentice House is the country's only campus-based, student-staffed book publishing company. Directed by professors and industry professionals, it is a nonprofit activity of the Communication Department at Loyola University Maryland.

Using state-of-the-art technology and an experiential learning model of education, Apprentice House publishes books in untraditional ways. This dual responsibility as publishers and educators creates an unprecedented collaborative environment among faculty and students, while teaching tomorrow's editors, designers, and marketers.

Outside of class, progress on book projects is carried forth by the AH Book Publishing Club, a co-curricular campus organization supported by Loyola University Maryland's Office of Student Activities.

Eclectic and provocative, Apprentice House titles intend to entertain as well as spark dialogue on a variety of topics. Financial contributions to sustain the press's work are welcomed. Contributions are tax deductible to the fullest extent allowed by the IRS.

To learn more about Apprentice House books or to obtain submission guidelines, please visit www.apprenticehouse.com.

Apprentice House
Communication Department
Loyola University Maryland
4501 N. Charles Street
Baltimore, MD 21210
Ph: 410-617-5265 • Fax: 410-617-2198
info@apprenticehouse.com • www.apprenticehouse.com

www.ingramcontent.com/pod-product-compliance
Lightning Source LLC
LaVergne TN
LVHW051521070426
835507LV00023B/3227